P9-BZS-545

ATWOOD

SURFACING

NOTES

COLES EDITORIAL BOARD

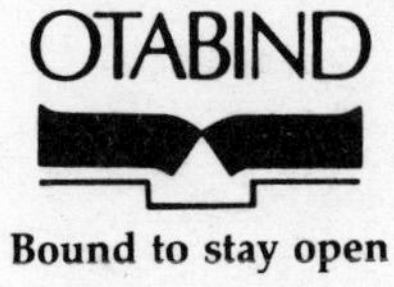

Publisher's Note

Otabind (Ota-bind). This book has been bound using the patented Otabind process. You can open this book at any page, gently run your finger down the spine, and the pages will lie flat.

ABOUT COLES NOTES

COLES NOTES have been an indispensible aid to students on five continents since 1948.

COLES NOTES are available for a wide range of individual literary works. Clear, concise explanations and insights are provided along with interesting interpretations and evaluations.

Proper use of COLES NOTES will allow the student to pay greater attention to lectures and spend less time taking notes. This will result in a broader understanding of the work being studied and will free the student for increased participation in discussions.

COLES NOTES are an invaluable aid for review and exam preparation as well as an invitation to explore different interpretive paths.

COLES NOTES are written by experts in their fields. It should be noted that any literary judgement expressed herein is just that – the judgement of one school of thought. Interpretations that diverge from, or totally disagree with any criticism may be equally valid.

COLES NOTES are designed to supplement the text and are not intended as a substitute for reading the text itself. Use of the NOTES will serve not only to clarify the work being studied, but should enhance the readers enjoyment of the topic.

ISBN 0-7740-3376-2

COLES PUBLISHING COMPANY
TORONTO - CANADA
PRINTED IN CANADA

Manufactured by Webcom Limited
Cover finish: Webcom's Exclusive **DURACOAT**

CONTENTS

Margaret Atwood: Life and Works

Certainly one of the most talked about Canadian writers, Margaret Atwood has been referred to as the "female star of Canada's literary elite," a "prophet in her own country," the "undisputed Queen of Canadian letters" and a "cult heroine." There has been a mythology built up around Atwood: everyone is fascinated by this woman who calls herself a "literary freak" and refers to her work as "rather quirky and eccentric." But the fascination does not end at the borders of Canada. Atwood is not only a bestselling author in her own country; the world-wide sales of her books are growing steadily. More than any other contemporary Canadian writer, Atwood has attracted the attention of readers and critics around the world.

Margaret Atwood was born in Ottawa in 1939, the second of three children, to parents of Nova Scotian background. Her father was an entomologist and Atwood spent the first five years of her life in the northern Quebec bush where he was employed by the federal government. She was greatly influenced by this experience and drew upon her knowledge of the northern bush in the writing of *Surfacing*. When she was seven years old, the family moved to Toronto where her father accepted a teaching offer from the University of Toronto. Her teenage years were spent in a middle-class suburb, and she worked as a camp counsellor and a resort waitress during the summers, which further broadened her interest in nature.

Although she wrote short stories and poems as a child, her first recognition as a writer came when she attended the University of Toronto. In 1959, while she was still an undergraduate, she published a poem in *Canadian Forum*. After winning a Woodrow Wilson Fellowship, she entered the graduate program at Harvard, emerging in 1962 with an M.A.. Atwood returned to Toronto in 1963 to work for a market research company and wrote a novel that was never published. During the next year, while teaching at the University of British Columbia, she wrote both *The Edible Woman* and *The Circle Game*, for which she won the Governor General's Award for poetry in 1966.

Atwood then returned to Harvard to work on a yet unfinished Ph.D. thesis before coming back to Canada to teach at Sir George Williams University. Her writing was becoming fruitful, with *Animals in That Country* appearing in 1968 and *The Edible*

Woman finally published in 1969, followed quickly by several books of poetry. As her reputation as a poet grew, she took time off from teaching in 1970 to travel to England, France and Italy, where she completed *Surfacing*. Returning once again to Canada, she became writer-in-residence at the University of Toronto in 1972.

Atwood has since travelled extensively, giving readings throughout Canada and around the world. An ex-editor at the House of Anansi Press, she remains very involved in the literary scene. In addition to her poetry, novels, short stories and screenplays — which have earned her the reputation of being a literary jack-of-all-trades — she has been active in the Writers' Union of Canada, serving terms as vice-president and president. Margaret Atwood presently lives near Toronto.

Major Works and Awards

Poetry:

Double Persephone	1961
The Circle Game	1966
The Animals in That Country	1968
The Journals of Susanna Moodie	1970
Procedures for Underground	1970
Power Politics	1971
You Are Happy	1974
Selected Poems	1976
Two-Headed Poems	1978
True Stories	1981

Fiction:

The Edible Woman	1969
Surfacing	1972
Lady Oracle	1976
Dancing Girls	1977
Life Before Man	1979
Bodily Harm	1981

Children's Books:

Up In the Tree	1978
Anna's Pet	1980

Non-Fiction:

Survival: A Thematic Guide to Canadian Literature	1972
Days of the Rebels: 1850-1840	1977
To See Our World	1980

Awards:

E.J. Pratt Medal	1961
President's Medal, University of Western Ontario	1965
Governor General's Award	1966
Centennial Commission Poetry Competition, First	1967
Union Poetry Prize, *Poetry*	1969
The Bess Hokins Prize, *Poetry*	1974
The City of Toronto Book Award	1977
The Canadian Bookseller's Association Award	1977
Periodical Distributors of Canada Short Fiction Award	1977
St. Lawrence Award for Fiction	1978
Canada Council Molson Prize	1980

Honourary Degrees:

Trent University	1973
Queen's University	1974
Concordia University	1979
Radcliffe Graduate Medal	1980

Introduction to *Surfacing*

To a large degree, Atwood's novels all deal with a similar situation: the problem of achieving a sense of wholeness and integrity in a modern, technological society. They are also very topical, being closely related to the times in which they were written. *The Edible Woman* reflects the conservatism of the late 50s and early 60s as the main character battles against consumerism and sexism. The late 60s and its concern with the environment, the growth of nationalism and the attempts of many to discover "true selfhood" emerge clearly in *Surfacing*. *Lady Oracle* is a product of the 70s, when society seemed to lose its sense of direction and enter a phase of confusion and apathy. Finally, both *Life Before Man* and *Bodily Harm* reflect the 80s, a time of revision of traditional roles and a time of concern about the death of individuals or of society. Yet, even though *Surfacing* contains elements found in Atwood's other novels — satire, topicality, the manipulation of traditional plot structures and black humour — it is certainly the most experimental in terms of its use of the language and the most ambitious in its scope.

Since it was first published in 1972, *Surfacing* has been the object of a great deal of critical controversy on an almost unknown level in Canada. Critical response has ranged from statements such as "one of the most important novels in the twentieth century," the "most intelligently poetic Canadian novel produced between 1960 and 1975," "an excellent novel, enriching, illuminating and beautiful" and "brilliant" to "a little banal," "drivel" and "a work of consistent and self-congratulatory feeblemindedness."

Although the majority of the critical response was full of praise, the debates did not end at general criticisms of the work. Feminists were concerned about the portrayal of abortion and Atwood's identification of the female body with nature. Other critics argued that *Surfacing* was simply a "souped-up demonstration model" or fictional counterpart to *Survival*, Atwood's critical work on Canadian literature. The controversy continues, but *Surfacing* seems destined to remain the object of literary acclaim for some time since, as one critic points out, "it speaks so [well] for a generation which is still fumbling for words, and it is rooted in the timeless regions of the psyche."

Characters in the Novel

Anna: David's wife. She is the narrator's best friend, although they have known each other only two months. Older than the narrator, she has been married to David for nine years. The marriage appears to be happy, but it is later revealed to be based on dependency, jealousy and hatred. A pathetic figure, Anna hides her true self behind a mask of resentful tolerance and makeup.

Claude: Son of the owner of the village motel and bar. He is a thin, "mottled" young man with an Elvis Presley haircut. In addition to helping his father run the bar, he works as a fishing guide.

David: Anna's husband. Although he teaches "Communications" and is the most talkative of the group, David never really seems to communicate with anyone, especially his wife. His interest in the trip lies in getting material for "Random Samples," an experimental movie he is making. A former theology student and radio announcer, he represents the more radical and ineffective nationalists in his vicious anti-Americanism. The oldest of the four, he is worried about aging.

Evans: Owner of the Blue Moon cabins. He is an old, "bulky laconic American" who works as a guide. The narrator hires him to take them to and from the cabin.

Joe: Narrator's current boyfriend. A failed potter who earns his living by teaching, Joe lives with the narrator in the city. He and the narrator seem distant from each other. Moody and withdrawn, Joe is the opposite of the talkative David. His silence and "furry" appearance link him with nature. More emotional than the narrator, he is deeply hurt by her refusal of his marriage proposal.

Madame: Paul's wife. Unlike her husband, she speaks only French. A stout woman, her appearance is typical of wood carvings sold in tourist handicraft shops.

Bill Malmstrom: A member of the Detroit branch of the Wildlife Protection Association of America. An executive type who tries to look like an authentic "woodsy" type. He makes an offer to buy the cabin so that his group can use it as a retreat. He appears to be a typical "American": the narrator distrusts him, and David suspects he is a CIA agent.

Narrator: The central character. A young commercial artist, she narrates the book from the first person point of view. However, her tendency to distort the truth makes her an unreliable narrator. She is an alienated person and cold-blooded in her response to others. She travels north in search of her missing father to the cabin where she spent much of her childhood. In the process of discovering the circumstances surrounding her father's death, she regains touch with her past and her hidden emotional life.

Narrator's Brother: As a baby, he once came close to drowning. The narrator seems fascinated by this event, even though it occurred several months before she was born. His personality is opposite to that of his sister. Attracted to science and violence from an early age, he complements her attraction to fantasy and passivity. He is out of touch with his family and works as a mineral rights explorer in Australia.

Narrator's Father: A "voluntary recluse," the narrator's father was a pacifist and a rationalist. A botanist and tree scientist by profession, he retired to the family cabin where he began studying Indian rock paintings. His disappearance is the reason for the narrator's trip, and his body is eventually found in the lake.

Narrator's "Husband": The narrator describes a failed marriage, ending in divorce. The wedding, held in a post office and conducted by a Justice of the Peace, is later revealed to be a lie. The narrator's former husband was, in fact, a "fake husband," her art teacher. Although she once worshipped him, she later realizes he was only an average, middle-aged man. The narrator also pretends that she had a child with him and which she left with him. She later reveals that their affair ended not in a birth but in an abortion.

Narrator's Mother: Now dead from cancer, the narrator's mother was afraid of hospitals and entered one only after she could no longer walk. The narrator remembers her as a lonely woman, mild-mannered and fond of birds and gardens. She was "either ten thousand years behind the rest or fifty years ahead." While her husband is associated with reason, she seems to represent emotion and natural cycles.

Paul: The narrator's father's best friend. Although he is French-Canadian, he speaks English. He discovers that the narrator's father is missing and notifies her. For her father, Paul represents the simple life and, like her mother, he is closely linked with nature and growing things.

Mr. Percival: The narrator's employer. As a publisher of children's books, he is a cautious man and avoids any book illustrations that he finds disturbing. Instead, he encourages the narrator to produce elegant, stylized drawings that often distort the meanings of the stories.

Plot Summary

The narrator, a woman in her late 20s who remains unnamed, returns to the isolated, northern cabin where she and her family had spent much of their time when she was a child. She is with her boyfriend, Joe, and a married couple, David and Anna. She has come to try and solve the mystery surrounding the disappearance of her father, who has been living alone in the cabin since the recent death of his wife. The narrator is convinced that her father is not dead, and she is determined to find him.

At the end of Part One, the narrator has not been able to find her father. Although she is now anxious to give up the search and return to the city, her friends decide to stay at the cabin for another week. While searching for clues to explain her father's disappearance, the narrator slowly grows closer to understanding what has happened to him. She discovers some drawings of ancient Indian rock paintings. Disguising the venture as a fishing excursion, she takes her friends on a short trip in the hope that she will be able to locate the original paintings.

During the fishing trip, all they discover is some American tourists and the body of a great blue heron, which the narrator believes the Americans have senselessly killed. She begins to dislike killing of any kind, and they return to the cabin. Determined to find the rock paintings, she then sets out alone and dives into the water where she thinks they might be.

Instead of discovering the paintings, the narrator finds the body of her father, trapped underwater by the weight of his camera. She does not recognize it as her father, however, and experiences a vision of a child that she had aborted several years earlier when she had an affair with a married man. She has been lying to others and to herself, claiming to have been married and to have left her child with her husband when she divorced him. Returning to the cabin, she reveals nothing of her discoveries to her friends and hides when they are preparing to return to the city. They leave without her and she goes through a series of visionary experiences, prompted by fasting and by what she believes to be a connection with ancient Indian gods. The novel ends with Joe coming back to search for her, and with the narrator, convinced that she is pregnant, trying to decide if she will return to the city with him.

Chapter by Chapter Summaries and Commentaries

NOTE: All quotations are from *Surfacing*, Margaret Atwood. PaperJacks, 1980.

PART ONE • CHAPTER 1

Summary

The narrator and central character of the novel is heading north with three friends. As they bypass a city, she remembers that as a child "I never thought of it as a city but as the last or first outpost." She remembers other features of the city: dreary restaurants with unappetizing food and the main street with its single movie theater.

The car they are travelling in belongs to David and Anna, her best friend and her friend's husband. Sitting in the back with her is her boyfriend, Joe.

The narrator is anxious; even though she has driven with her friends before, "on this road it doesn't seem right, either the three of them are in the wrong place or I am." Her vague fears are in contrast to the holiday mood of Anna and David, who are whistling and singing old songs. We learn that the narrator's father is missing.

David and Joe are making a movie they intend to call "Random Samples." Even though they have never made one before, Joe is doing all the camera work, and David is directing the movie. They want shots of interesting things they happen to see, and the narrator shows them "bottle villa," a house made of pop bottles cemented together.

As they cross the border, marked by a sign that has *Welcome* on one side and *Bienvenue* on the other, the narrator states that "now we're on my home ground, foreign territory." Her nervousness increases and her throat becomes constricted. They drive into the company town, which smells of sawdust from the paper mill, and the narrator find herself lost. The road that she remembers is now blocked and, since they didn't bring a map, she gets directions from a store owner. The detour they must make upsets the narrator. Shaking, she realizes that "nothing is the same, I don't know the way anymore."

David and Anna continue to make comments and tell

jokes, unaware that the narrator is fighting back tears. The attention of the group is caught by three stuffed moose dressed in human clothes, standing up on their back legs in front of a gas station. The narrator, embarrassed by both her friends and the moose, explains that the display wasn't there before.

As they drive down the new road, the narrator notices a roadside crucifix that has a wooden Christ, "the alien god, mysterious to me as ever." Seeing the old road crossing in front of them, the narrator remembers driving down it with her family, whom she refers to as "they." Suddenly she realizes "that won't work; I can't call them 'they' as if they were someone else's family. I have to keep myself from telling that story." Shortly after the new road turns from pavement into gravel and joins the old road, they pass by blasted rocks and cliffs painted with graffiti and advertisements. Though she had felt ill for a moment, the narrator is shocked that she has reached the village without being carsick.

Commentary

The opening chapter introduces us not only to the central characters of *Surfacing*, but to the themes, ideas and tone of the work. Of prime importance is the voice of the narrator. Written in the first person, this book is narrated by a narrator whose perceptions effect all her observations and comments. This is not a factual, unbiased record of a journey; this is a personal, and therefore somewhat distorted, view of a certain set of experiences.

The first sentence highlights the anxious tone in this chapter. The narrator is experiencing fear that cannot be accounted for. She seems alienated from Joe and is nervous that he has caught her looking at him. David's movie-making and anti-American comments unnerve her, and she and Anna seem distant from one another.

The intrusion of memories from the past sets up the tension between "then" and "now" that is developed throughout the novel. When they cross the border into "home ground," a place she knew well in the past, it is at the same time "foreign territory." The area is foreign not just because it is French-speaking but because, like the past, she has not kept in touch with it; things have changed. Most significant is the fact that the narrator, the one responsible for guiding the others through this "foreign territory," gets lost herself. The original way is "blocked"; she has to ask directions and journey on a new road to the past. Her father's comment that "there was nothing in the north but the past" takes on a more personal meaning for her. When she is confused about the direction and has to go a different way, her reaction is fear. She wants to turn around and go back to the city and never find out what happened to him.

Anna's comments about the double lines in the narrator's palms reinforce this tension between the present and the past by introducing the idea of the narrator's divided self. She does not have a twin, but she does seem to have a double life: her present life and her past life. Other dualities introduced in the first chapter are: north/south, wilderness/city, French/English and American/Canadian.

CHAPTER 2

Summary

As they pull into the village, the narrator notices a new motel and bar. Since she has to inquire about her father in the village, she leaves Joe, David and Anna at the bar. She likes and trusts her friends, but she wishes they hadn't accompanied her. She suspects that her concern for her father embarrasses them.

She passes a dam that controls the lakes, and it triggers a memory from her childhood. She and her parents were canoeing out to their cabin in a thick fog when they realized they had lost direction and were nearing some rapids. What the narrator remembers most clearly is a feeling of total safety. She realizes that she did have a happy childhood, after all. Even though she was raised in the middle of the war, she had no knowledge of it until later and "at the time it felt like peace."

Walking through the village which, unlike other things, is unchanged, she reaches Paul's house. Paul, a French-Canadian who speaks English, is her father's best friend. Paul represents the simple life her father sought. The narrator is annoyed that he and his wife both resemble carvings, the type they sell in tourist handicraft shops. She also realizes, however, that dressed so casually, she must look odd to them.

Paul does not recognize her at first but realizes who she is when she thanks him for writing to her of her father's disappearance. Although Paul's letter seemed incredible at the time, she now recognizes that it appears to be true. She learns from Paul that her father has not returned, and Paul describes the searches that he and the police have conducted. Despite indications to the contrary, however, the narrator thinks they may have missed something in their searches and is convinced that she will discover something. She feels there is a good chance that when they get to the cabin, her father will have returned.

While she has tea with Paul and his wife, the narrator remembers her parents' visits with them. Her father and Paul would talk and exchange vegetables from their gardens. Her mother and Paul's wife would struggle to engage in conversation, even though neither spoke the other's language. The narrator also recalls her mother's painful death. She visited her in the hospital and left with her mother's diary, hoping to find something about herself in it. However, the diary only contained observations on the weather.

Paul asks if her husband is with her, and she lies and says yes. She is still wearing her wedding ring, even though she is divorced and her child is living with her former husband. Her parents received only a postcard regarding the wedding and no notice of the divorce. As far as anyone knows, the narrator is still married. A memory of her former husband intrudes, but she avoids thinking of him: "I don't have time for him, I switch problems."

Commentary

The narrator's memory of her family's fearful experience in the canoe is a curious one. She remembers feeling not fear but trust and safety. She also states that she trusts her friends, but the statement is suspicious in light of her actions. She does not trust them to behave appropriately, and at a time when she is likely in need of support, she does not confide in them about her feelings. Also curious is the fact that during the war she felt she was living in a time of peace.

The pattern of dualities introduced in the first chapter is continued here. The tension between the French and English arises again when she meets with Paul, a French-Canadian who speaks English, and when she attempts to talk with his wife, who speaks only French. While Paul and his wife seem to be a typical French-Canadian couple, the narrator appears to be a typical, contemporary English woman, with jeans, a sweatshirt and a fringed bag. The barometer couple she remembers in Paul's house introduces the male/female duality: two wooden figures moving in opposite directions.

The fact that Paul does not recognize her is of significance. Throughout the first two chapters the narrator finds things she doesn't recognize or remember: roads, landmarks and curiosities like the stuffed moose. Now, when she begins to recognize the village, the village doesn't recognize her. She has been away too long; she has changed.

Also of significance is the fact she lies about Joe, calling him her husband. The reader places his trust in the narrator. If she is shown to be a person who deceives people, she may be an untrustworthy narrator.

The narrator is involved in a mystery; she is attempting to discover what has happened to her father. She looks for clues about her father when she asks Paul questions, but she also looks for clues about other things. She searches for references about herself in her mother's diary, and she looks to the barometer for an answer: "I need a prediction." These are also clues for the reader since they indicate that there is more than a mystery to be solved in *Surfacing*.

CHAPTER 3

Summary

After leaving Paul and his wife, the narrator finds a store where she can buy some food. The woman behind the counter and some men in the store stop what they're doing and stare at her. Unsure if they will understand English, she attempts to order in French but her efforts are mocked by the people in the store. She has forgotten that "this is border country."

As she leaves, she remembers a store that was in the village when she was young. The narrator remembers being fascinated by the old woman who ran the store because she was missing a hand. The narrator found the stump "a great mystery, almost as puzzling as Jesus." Although she was curious about the missing hand, she recalls that she "never asked, I must have been afraid of the answers."

She meets up with her friends in the bar where she left them and joins them for a beer. The bar is "an imitation of other places, more southern ones" with its carved fish and angling pictures on the walls. David begins to tell her about the conversation he has had with Claude, the owner's son, and the narrator listens to him "slipping into his yokel dialect." Although he usually does it to parody the way he was when he sold bibles door to door, she wonders if he is now trying to impress Claude with his manner of talking.

Joe asks if there is any news of her father, and the narrator explains in a calm, level voice that there is none. Recalling the first time she and Joe made love, the narrator remembers that she didn't just act coolly but actually didn't feel any emotions. Her "coolness" arises again when she resolves that if her father is safe, "I don't want to see him." She is convinced her parents never forgave her for either her divorce or leaving her child.

The narrator informs her friends that she would like to go down to the lake for a few days to look around, and they agree. The narrator hires a guide named Evans to take them to the lake and pick them up later. The journey to her parents' cabin is a strange one. It begins to rain, and the shoreline looks like a "tangled maze." The narrator knows the weather is unpredictable and the lake is tricky, and "because of the convolutions it's easy to lose the way if you haven't memorized the landmarks." Although she doesn't trust Evans and watches for the landmarks, he does manage to get them to the cabin, after entering what the narrator calls "my territory." As they approach the cabin, the narrator remembers an event that happened just before she was born: her brother's near death from drowning in the water around the dock. Her mother was pregnant with her at the time, and the narrator imagines that even as an unborn baby she could see through to the outside world.

Commentary

The narrator is taking on the role not only of organizer but also of protector. She leaves her friends in a bar while she goes by herself to find out information about her father. She takes it upon herself to go through the embarrassing confrontations that occur when she tries to buy supplies. She even remembers to buy insect repellent for her city friends. They are not exposed to the difficulties of communicating with French-Canadians and neither are they exposed to a display of the narrator's feelings now that the disappearance of her father seems certain.

This protectiveness is partly responsible for the alienation existing between the narrator and her friends. Her reluctance to reveal her feelings regarding her present ordeal, and the memory of her lack of emotion after she and Joe made love, point to a woman who is lacking in both emotions and in an ability to express what feelings she has. Significantly, she notes that "my friends' pasts are vague to me and to each other also, any one of us could have amnesia for years and the others wouldn't notice." The four friends are as distant from one another as the narrator is from them.

Her difficulties in the store remind us of the continuing tension existing between the French-speaking and the English-speaking people. She realizes too late that she should not have attempted to speak French. She should have pretended to be an American tourist since this is "border country."

Her memory of the one-handed woman is significant, especially since she remembers that the reason she never asked questions about the hand was because she was afraid of the answers. Similarly, when Paul indicated to her in the previous chapter that her father is definitely missing and perhaps dead, she felt confident that he had returned and would be waiting for them in the cabin. She does not seem to want to know the truth about what has happened to him.

Also of significance are the narrator's thoughts and observations of the boat trip to the cabin. The journey motif introduced in the first chapter is picked up again, and the tone of fear and confusion also reappears. Just as the drive to the village was complicated by detours, new roads and different landmarks, so the trip to the cabin is confusing and eerie. The description of the landscape, the winding waterways, sheer cliffs and decaying logs, all evoke a particular mood. The narrator feels lost and helpless, walking in circles in the "tangled maze" that the mystery of her father's disappearance is becoming.

CHAPTER 4

Summary

Evans gets them to the cabin and after they unload their bags and pay him, he leaves. The lake seems very quiet after the journey getting there. The narrator feels the urge to announce their arrival by shouting, but doesn't.

The cabin has changed over the years. It seems smaller

because the trees are bigger. Her father built it of upright cedar logs, and they have turned grey because they are beginning to decay. The sandhill that the cabin is built on is held down by only a few inches of soil and some trees and is crumbling away on one side. The first fireplace the family used is gone, and many trees are in the process of falling down. The chicken-wire fence that her brother stayed inside as a baby and an old swing still exist, but they are in a state of disrepair. The narrator notices evidence of erosion and decay everywhere she looks. She thinks guiltily of her child and of her failure to provide her parents with grandchildren, "a dynasty."

They all enter the cabin, and the narrator looks for anything that might indicate where her father is. The rooms are plain and simply furnished: a main room that serves as a kitchen and livingroom, and two bedrooms. In one of the bedrooms is a map, in the other are pictures that the narrator painted as a child. When she recognizes them, she feels uneasy because she had forgotten about them.

As she begins to prepare dinner, she notices that Joe looks worried. She wonders if "perhaps he's been expecting me to have hysterics and he's anxious because I'm not having any." When Anna asks her if she's okay, the narrator is surprised by the question and displays no worry or grief. She is concerned about reassuring and comforting her friends.

While in the garden, the narrator recalls that, as a child, she thought that certain beans were the source of a mysterious power. She thinks that it is fortunate she never got this power since "if I'd turned out like the others with power I would have been evil." She also recalls her brother's early obsession with moral distinctions. She remembers that for him, "there had to be a good kind and a bad kind of everything."

After supper, when they are looking for things to do, the narrator finds her father's books, several of which are written by 18th century rationalists like Boswell, Goldsmith and Cowper. He was an admirer of these men, and he was interested in their search for a balanced life.

The four friends decide to spend the evening sitting on the dock, drinking beer, smoking pot and telling jokes. Even though the narrator is critical of her friends, she is glad of their presence. She wouldn't want to be alone.

While sitting with her friends, the narrator reflects on her own brief and unsuccessful marriage. She regrets having married her husband since it seems that the "paper act" of marriage was what changed him into a more demanding man and destroyed their relationship. She thinks Anna and David's marriage is successful because they have "some special method, formula, some knowledge I missed out on."

Commentary

The narrator continues to think about her ex-husband and child. Her explanation for why she never brought the child to visit her parents is confusing. She claims that the child was always her husband's, that she never identified it as hers. Her guilt about not creating the dynasty that her father would have wanted seems to be relieved by describing the child as never really belonging to her. Similarly, when she recalls her failed marriage, she blames the actual marriage ceremony. Significantly, she remembers thinking at the time that the perfect marriage "would happen without my doing anything about it."

Just as she evades the responsibility for her child and her marriage, so the narrator alienates herself from her friends and her boyfriend. She continues to avoid revealing her feelings, even when her friends express their concern about her. She remains a cool, detached woman in the middle of an agonizing situation. She avoids any real emotional closeness with her friends or with Joe. If you do not become close with someone, you will not be hurt by them. If you are not sure how they feel and do not ask, you cannot be made to feel responsible for their feelings. When Joe is on the dock, the narrator admits that his rocking back and forth may mean he's happy. She is not sure and by not asking, she is therefore protected from responsibility for either his unhappiness or happiness.

The search for clues that we saw in Chapter 3 continues in this chapter. The narrator remains detached about her search for her father. Even as she looks for answers, she is afraid of finding the truth. She wants to call out when she arrives, but doesn't because she is afraid that the answer will be silence. She approaches the cabin with fear since "whatever I find inside will be a clue." Nothing is out of place in the cabin, however, and she finds no evidence that will explain her father's absence. She sees some papers and wonders if there might be a note, a message or a will, but she doesn't look through them.

CHAPTER 5

Summary

It is the morning of the second day, and the narrator wakes up early. Joe has not slept well, waking up in the middle of the night not knowing where he was or who he was with. He is asleep now, and the narrator observes him. Once again, she compares him to an animal. She describes the hair on his back as being like fur.

She wonders about their relationship; she is unsure whether she loves him or not. She does not wonder about this because she is confused or curious, but because she suspects that he will ask her soon, and she wants to have the answer worked out in advance. She analyzes their relationship in a very cold manner, summing him up by "dividing him into categories." She recalls that her decision to live with him was not a real decision but "was more like buying a goldfish or a potted cactus plant." She realizes that although she is fond of him, he doesn't mean very much to her. She has not cared deeply for anyone since her husband.

Looking at the drawings of ladies in exotic costumes that she drew when she was young, she remembers that "when I was ten I believed in glamour, it was a kind of religion and those were my icons." Glamour no longer holds the same meaning for her. After she gets up to start the fire, she meets Anna in the kitchen putting on her makeup. Without makeup, Anna's face is "curiously battered, a worn doll's, her artificial face is the natural one." The narrator finds out that David doesn't know Anna wears makeup, and she is afraid to be seen without it. The narrator is not sure whether Anna's makeup involves deceit or devotion. She later asks Anna how she and David manage to stay together, thinking there might be a secret "trick" to it. Anna tells her that you have to make an emotional commitment and "let go." Later, when the narrator thinks about her husband, she is surprised by the bitterness that accompanies the memory. He kept repeating that he loved her, and the narrator realizes that she'll never trust that word again.

After breakfast, the group departs on a search of a trail that runs along the shore of the island. The narrator thinks that her father might have followed it to get some wood. Since the canoes and the motorboat are still there, she decides that there are only two places he can be, on the island or in the lake. Even as she says this, however, she realizes that someone might have picked him up and taken him to the village, or he may never have been here during the winter at all. She recognizes that she's only avoiding the problem by thinking of these other explanations, but she can't accept the idea that he got lost in the woods.

The trail soon becomes difficult to follow as the forest thickens. It becomes dense, like a jungle, and she decides to turn back. Even though he could be in the woods, she recognizes that it is impossible for the four of them to search the whole island. She also wonders if he might be hiding somewhere, avoiding anyone who is searching for him.

Commentary

It becomes clear in this chapter that the narrator's alienation from Joe stems not only from an evasion of responsibility but also from what appears to be a lack of emotions. Although she is fond of him, she says it would be nice if he meant something more. Significantly, it is also revealed that the narrator doesn't have dreams any longer. It is as if, in Anna's words, the narrator simply doesn't "let go."

The idea of fragmentation, central to the narrator's problem of a "divided self," is highlighted in this chapter. She says of her separation from her husband: "a divorce is like an amputation, you survive, but there's less of you." She is less than she was, and what seems to have been destroyed or lost is her ability to feel. Similarly, when she reflects upon her child, she feels she must behave as if it doesn't exist. Even though she was the one who left her child, she describes the separation as if someone else had imposed it upon her. Once again, the narrator evades responsibility for her actions. Significantly, she also describes the separation from her child in very personal, physical terms: "a section of my own life, sliced off from me like a Siamese twin, my own flesh cancelled." As in her divorce, she survives, but there is less of her. Something is missing; she is incomplete.

The physical journey introduced in the beginning chapters is now moving towards a physical search for her father. The narrator continues to look for clues to her father's whereabouts. Although she says that he can only be on the island or in the lake, she begins to think of other possibilites. He could have been taken away by someone, he might not have been there to begin with, or strangest of all, he might be hiding. She wonders if she should have checked to see how old the garbage was but doesn't, even though this might reveal how recent his disappearance was.

The search on the trail becomes increasingly difficult. The narrator acts like a detective faced with a mystery. She looks for footprints and broken branches but finally admits defeat. Her father could be alive or dead, but she either cannot find the evidence or the clues are too confusing. The narrator also avoids investigating certain clues, as if here, too, she wishes to avoid responsibility. It is as if, once again, she will not ask because she is afraid of the answer.

CHAPTER 6

Summary

The narrator decides that she has done all she can to find her father. To search any further would be a waste of time. There is nothing to do now but wait until tomorrow when Evans will pick them up and go back to the city.

David and Joe have taken the canoes and although it's cool out, Anna is sunbathing and reading a murder mystery. The narrator decides to work on some of the drawings that she has brought with her. She never intended to be a commercial artist or an illustrator. When she revealed to her husband that she wanted to be a real artist, however, he talked her out of it, pointing out that there have never been any important female artists.

The book she's working on is called *Quebec Folk Tales*. It isn't the kind of book she usually illustrates, but she agreed to do it because she needed the money. The stories are strange; they are like German fairy tales but with less violence. The narrator has learned to avoid anything frightening in her drawings and now draws what the publisher wants. She begins to work on an illustration for a story called "The Tale of the Golden Phoenix" but is not satisfied with the drawing she produces.

She wonders if the people who live in the village near the island ever knew the stories she is working on. She realizes that she didn't know what the villagers thought or talked about, for she was so shut off from them. Recalling her childhood fascination with religion, she remembers that her father reluctantly allowed her to attend Sunday School. As a rationalist, he "wished to protect us from its distortions." Although she attended a United Church, she soon lost interest and decided she would rather be a Catholic, until her brother told her bizarre stories about Catholicism.

She wonders if the villagers think her father has turned into a wolf. This thought triggers a reflection upon Joe, and she realizes that "everything I value about him seems to be physical, the rest is either unknown, disagreeable or ridiculous." She doesn't seem to have a lot of respect for his pottery, which he mutilates by bending after he shapes it. She concludes finally that "perhaps it's not only his body I like, perhaps it's his failure; that also has a kind of purity."

After Anna comes in and asks the narrator what her father was doing in the cabin, the narrator feels angry with him for vanishing, leaving her with no answers to give to anyone who asks. She never found it strange that her father stayed alone in the cabin since he had always preferred to be away from "irrational" humans and closer to animals.

The narrator finally takes down the stack of papers she had noticed when she first arrived. She realizes she has been avoiding them, but now that she is sure he's dead, she feels she should examine them. She expects botany reports but instead discovers drawings, numbers and notations. She can't make sense of them and hides them from her friends. Now the narrator is faced with another possibility: her father may have gone insane and spent the winter making strange drawings.

Commentary

The chapter opens with a revealing statement from the narrator: "No one can expect anything else from me, I checked everything, I tried; now I'm absolved from knowing." The reader will see that, although the narrator has tried, she has not tried everything. She has not, for example, examined the garbage nor has she, at this point, examined the stack of papers left behind by her father. Because the reader sees that the narrator is making a statement that is not true, he sees that the narrator is not wholly reliable. Also of significance in the opening sentence is the narrator's statement that she is absolved, not from guilt, but from knowing. Once again, we find the narrator avoiding questions because of her fear of the answers.

The folk tale she is working on is also of interest. The phoenix is the traditional symbol of renewal and rebirth. Ovid, the Latin poet and author of *Metamorphoses*, records the legend of the phoenix in which he describes how the bird lives for five centuries of its life and then burns itself on a pyre. From its ashes, another phoenix emerges, which will live for another five centuries. Since the narrator is searching for clues about not only her father's disappearance but also the "death" of her emotional life, this symbol will gather increasing importance as the novel proceeds.

Her decision to look at her father's papers is a crucial one. She states that after the search in the bush, she has finally admitted to herself that he is dead and feels it is now acceptable for her to examine what he may have left for her. But she has not really accepted his death; she just doesn't want to look anymore. Her reaction to the drawings is swift and intense, the strongest reaction she has had to anything since her anxiousness in the car on the trip to the village. First, she hides the papers, not wanting her friends to share her discovery. Once again, she distances herself from them at a time when it would seem that she needs them most. Secondly, she comes to the conclusion that he is insane. Curiously, she describes her reaction in the following way: "my heart speeded up as if I've opened what I thought was an empty closet and found myself face to face with a thing that isn't supposed to be there." The expression this statement echoes is "skeletons in the closet," a phrase used to indicate dark secrets in a person's past that he wants to keep hidden from others. Thus, Atwood neatly foreshadows what the reader will eventually discover about the truth of the narrator's past.

CHAPTER 7

Summary

Since it is the last night they will spend at the cabin and they have not yet been fishing, the narrator organizes a trip for her friends. She gathers worms from the garden, advises David on what fishing rod and tackle to use, and even puts the bait on his hook for him.

Anna wants to stay behind and read, but the narrator lies and says she needs Anna in the canoe for extra weight. The canoe is actually too full with the four of them in it, but she is worried about leaving Anna alone. If her father is still on the island, he may return to the cabin.

The narrator feels sure that her father will keep away if the four of them are together, but she is still worried when they are in the canoe. As they move away from the shoreline, she is relieved because he can't follow them out there.

Her attention is diverted for a moment by a blue heron flying overhead. Its call is a "rasping pterodactyl croak," and she remembers that there was once a colony of herons on the lake.

David is unsuccessful using the worms as bait, and she decides to let him use a frog. Anna calls her cold-blooded when she puts the frog on the hook, not realizing that the narrator never had to do this before since someone else always did it for her. The narrator stares into the water, meditating, remembering that as a child she used to pretend that the fish she caught were willing: "they had chosen to die and forgiven me in advance."

The frog proves to be a successful bait, and David hooks a walleye pickerel. Since David doesn't manage to kill the fish properly, the narrator must do this as well. She is sickened by the sight of the dead fish because she realizes that she's actually killed something. Because of her father's influence, however, the narrator realizes that it is "irrational" to feel badly since killing certain things, like food and enemies, is all right.

Just before they decide to stop fishing, a big powerboat with American flags on it pulls in beside them. The narrator feels that the Americans are a menace and about as friendly as sharks. Even though she used to think of Americans as harmless and even "faintly loveable, like President Eisenhower," she now sees them as a threat to the environment: "they're the kind who catch more than they can eat and they'd do it with dynamite if they could get away with it."

As they return to the cabin, the narrator relaxes. She muses that "being here feels right to me for the first time, and I know it's because we're leaving tomorrow." Madness is a private thing, she feels, and her father should be left alone. She decides to burn his drawings before they leave, because "they're evidence of the wrong sort."

Commentary

Even though the evidence is slim — a brief glance at a collection of drawings — the narrator seems convinced that her father is alive and insane and roaming the island. She is sure that he'll keep away if the four of them stay together, but she bases this on the fact that he never liked crowds. Even when the four are together in the canoe, she shows her paranoia by thinking "he can't follow us here." Her fear seems erratic and without much of a logical basis. Also suspicious is the fact that, whereas before she was willing to leave because she was sure he was dead, now she is anxious to leave the island even though she is confident that he is alive.

The narrator is definitely the organizing figure in the fishing trip, even though she does not enjoy either baiting the hooks or killing the fish. Her saying to the fish "please be caught," seems to be more of a way of excusing her guilt than of attracting the fish to the hook. Similarly, she lessens her guilt over killing the fish by telling herself that sometimes killing is all right. This rationalization points to another important dualism that Atwood presents to the reader: reason and emotion. The narrator *feels* that it is wrong to kill the fish, but she *thinks* that it is justifiable.

The concept of rationalization emerges once again in the narrator's statement regarding the reason why it is now appropriate to leave the island. She says that she will leave because her father, in his madness, has the right to privacy. The reader must now wonder if her reason for wanting to leave is that she wants to avoid the problems that staying on the island present to her: confrontation with not only her father but also her past.

CHAPTER 8

Summary

In the early morning of the next day, the last day at the cabin, Joe wakes the narrator and they make love. Their responses seem calculated and no emotions are expressed.

Later, the narrator is preparing the fish for breakfast, and

David decides that it would be interesting to include some shots of it in his movie. While he and Joe are filming the fish entrails, the narrator thinks about her mother's photo album, where there are "successive incarnations of me preserved and flattened like flowers pressed in dictionaries."

Evans will be coming for them soon, so the narrator begins packing after they finish breakfast. She wonders if she should take the bedding and towels since no one will be living there now. If her father decides not to return, she is responsible for the cabin since her brother does not keep in touch with the family. The brother lives in Australia where he works as a prospector for an international company.

She overhears David and the others say that they would like to stay at the cabin, and the narrator immediately begins thinking of ways to talk them out of it. She doesn't feel she could tell them about her father, since that would be betraying him, and also they might think she was making it up. The other two excuses she comes up with — her work and a lack of food — are obvious lies, and she is forced to allow them to stay.

When Evans arrives and David and Joe go down to talk with him, the narrator goes to the outhouse and begins thinking of the times she spent in cities as a child. Her family lived in a different city each year, and she spent her childhood isolated from other children. They thought of her as a "hermit crab" and she always felt like a person from another culture. She became an "escape artist" at getting free of skipping ropes other children would tie her up with, and she remembers praying to be made invisible.

Thinking about the cabin, she remembers that she always felt safe there. Suddenly, she realizes that's actually a lie, and a moment of panic sets in. She thinks for a while about her memories:

> I have to be more careful about my memories, I have to be sure they're my own and not the memories of other people telling me what I felt, how I acted, what I said: if the events are wrong the feelings I remember about them will be wrong too, I'll start inventing them and there will be no way of correcting it, the ones who could help are gone. I run quickly over my

> version of it, my life, checking it like an alibi; it fits, it's all there till the time I left. (p. 78)

She can remember the past, at least one version of it, but she can't seem to remember what happened after she left home. Trying not to panic, she begins repeating her name like a chant until a knock on the door breaks the mood and calms her down.

This chapter marks the end of Part One with the narrator pushing herself reluctantly into the lake for a swim.

Commentary

The chapter opens with another forceful example of the narrator's coldness. She describes her lovemaking with Joe by focussing on the actions of his hands: "they repeat patterns he's tried before, they've found out what works." She responds the same way, "educated, crisp as a typewriter." The scene is described with no references to emotions, especially love. The narrator sounds as if she were speaking of machines. The idea of anonymity also arises when she states that "it's the best when you don't know them." The high school joke about two people making love with paper bags over their heads highlights her impersonal reactions and observations.

As her memories of the past intrude with increasing frequency, so does the occurrence of lies and deceptions. She thinks of several lies to present to her friends in order to convince them not to stay. Most significant, however, is the lie she unintentionally tells herself. When she realizes that remembering the time spent at the cabin as a time in which she was never afraid is a lie, she panics. Terrified of losing control, she realizes that she has to be more careful with her memories. She has to be sure they are accurate or the feeling she remembers experiencing will be incorrect. She is afraid that she will start inventing memories. As if rehearsing, she goes over what she calls a "version of it, my life." In calling her memories a "version," the narrator indirectly hints that even these memories are probably inaccurate. At this point, the reader may well suspect that many of the memories the narrator has recalled in previous chapters may not be truthful accounts of the past. A narrator who lies, especially to herself and especially when she does not mean to, is not a narrator to be trusted.

Since the title of the book implies both diving down and

resurfacing, the narrator's dive into the lake at the end of this chapter is important. Although she often used to swim in the lake as a child, this is the first time she has entered the water since her arrival at the cabin. It is not an enjoyable dive into the lake; the narrator must force herself to enter the water. It is important to note that this action concludes Part One, and its symbolic implications are important to the development of the novel. Water has long been the traditional symbol of both rebirth and the unconscious. This action, therefore, signals a dramatic change in the development of the narrator and of the plot.

PART TWO • CHAPTER 9

Summary

Chapter 9 marks the beginning of Part Two and also brings a change in tense. Throughout Part One, everything but actual memories of her childhood and her marriage is narrated in the present tense. Now everything is narrated in the past tense.

The chapter opens with the narrator sitting in a darkened bedroom, listening to her friends play cards. She is upset, and her thoughts are bizarre. She begins with a theory that if humans did not have a neck, they would not experience the problem of the separation of the head from the body. This separation poses a dangerous problem since it encourages people to move their bodies "as if they were robots or puppets." She isn't sure when she first suspected that she had this problem and that her friends were beginning to have it as well. Listening to them in the other room, however, she describes them as if they were machines: "canned laughter, they carry it with them, the midget reels of tape and the on switch concealed somewhere in their chests, instant playback." She feels as if she didn't notice the transformation because she was "seeing poorly, translating badly, a dialect problem." Now, however, she has "the clues and solutions and the power for what I must do."

She is uneasy after Evans leaves because of her fear of her father. She feels as if the island isn't safe, and they are trapped on it. The others don't seem to be aware of the threat, and the narrator feels responsible for them. She senses his presence and is certain that he is watching them, "ready to pounce or take flight." Although he might be harmless, she feels she has to keep her friends out of danger.

When David and Joe decide to chop some wood for the stove, she allows them to go into the bush only because there is more than one of them, and they could use their axes as weapons. She and Anna decide to work in the garden. The narrator feels that it's important to keep busy; they must preserve the signs of order. She tries to conceal her fear, both from the others and from him. As they work, she checks now and then to see if her father has approached them from the forest.

Anna breaks the silence by asking the narrator if she uses birth control pills. The narrator begins to think about birth control, remembering that "love without fear, sex without risk, that was what they wanted to be true, and they almost did it." This leads her to a memory of giving birth to her child, which she describes in a very strange manner. She is bitter that her husband was not there for the birth since she feels the experience was "his idea, his fault."

Commentary

As the beginning of Part Two, this chapter is a dramatic turning point in the novel with regard to plot and characterization. Reinforcing the importance of this chapter is the change in tense from the present to the past. The change is deliberate and consistent — all of Part Two is narrated in the past tense. Atwood is alerting the reader, telling him to pay close attention because important changes will soon take place.

As the reader begins his detective work, one of the changes he will observe is that the narrator is becoming increasingly concerned with the past — her past. It will no longer be enough just to remember events, now the narrator must try and understand them. She has finally recognized that something is wrong with her. She feels as if her head and her body have become separated. Her emotions and her intellect are no longer connected. She is acting as if she has no emotions; she is acting like a robot. The narrator recognizes the seriousness of this condition when she realizes that "if the head is detached from the body both of them will die." She must re-examine her past — a time when she still had emotions — in order to achieve unity between her mind and her body. Previously, she has been "seeing poorly, translating badly." Now she must take the "clues and solutions and the power" she feels she has and try other methods to help herself. Inside her and her past are the clues and the evidence.

Language does not seem to be the proper way to accomplish this. The narrator realizes she should have invented another language to help her with this problem. Significantly, she reminds the reader of Joe's problem with language: "speech to him was a task, a battle, words mustered behind his beard and issued one at a time, heavy and square like tanks."

The narrator's paranoia about her father continues to grow. Concern about his well-being has turned to fear, and she is certain that he is watching them from the woods. As always, she hides her fear from the others, choosing to protect them without letting them know that she thinks they are in danger. However, the reader must once again question the narrator's fear. What is she basing this fear on? What evidence does she have that her father is alive? The drawings seem to be weak evidence of her certainty that he is alive and mad.

Finally, the narrator's description of the birth of her child poses problems for the reader. Records of giving birth are often strange and sometimes violent, but the narrator's description seems to be particularly odd. For example, why does she suggest that she went through this ordeal for nothing when she has previously said that she gave birth to a healthy child?

CHAPTER 10

Summary

The next day the narrator is still feeling trapped. They have five more days to spend at the cabin, and she is just counting the days until they can leave. Her fear of her father is still evident. She reasons that the fact he had not yet appeared only increased the possibility that he would. However, her fear seems to be directed not only at her father but for him. She wants to get her friends away from the island "to protect them from him, to protect him from them, save all of them from knowledge."

Afraid that her friends might want to go off exploring around the island, the narrator arranges a trip to another island to pick blueberries. They go by a cluster of tiny islands while they are in the canoes, one of which is a nesting ground for the heron colony. While they are picking blueberries, she remembers that, as a child, she used to see a native Indian family who picked blueberries on the islands. They were the last Indian family on the lake. She remembers their faces as being neutral and distanced, and that they never spoke with or came near her family. She is surprised to realize that "it never occurred to me until now that they must have hated us."

Joe, who has been moody and thoughtful, suddenly asks the narrator to marry him. She is shocked and tries not to laugh. She argues that it isn't necessary since they are already living together, but he insists. When she refuses, he says, "I get the feeling you don't give a shit about me." The narrator insists that she does, wondering "if that was the equivalent of saying I loved him." Meanwhile, she starts planning to move out on him, figuring out how much money she has and how long it would take her to pack. She sees his proposal as a threat, as if he is only asking her so that she will give in, and he will win a battle of wills.

She begins to panic when he becomes not angry but sad. He is becoming, as she says, "three-dimensional." To help explain her reaction, she begins to tell him about her marriage and her child. Her explanation, however, sounds very robot-like: "the words were coming out of me like the mechanical words from a talking doll, the kind with the pull tape at the back; the whole speech was unwinding, everything in order, a spool."

The memory of her wedding that follows is very strange. It took place in a post office, and she remembers a number of strange smells, including antiseptic. When the ceremony was over, her husband behaved as if she were an invalid, not a bride. He asked her if she was feeling better, and she could hardly stand because her legs were shaking. He said, "I know it's tough, but it's better this way."

Later that night, she goes into one of the bedrooms and discovers some things that were out of place: a photo album, some unused wedding presents of her mother's and some scrapbooks. Although she feels as if she was opening someone else's private diary, she looks through her brother's scrapbook. It is full of pictures of war, comic book heroes and explorers. Her scrapbook contains none of this violence; it is full of pictures of ladies. She looks through hers carefully, looking for something she could recognize as herself, clues to where she had come from or gone wrong. She finds an earlier scrapbook of hers filled with drawings of ornately-decorated Easter eggs with people shaped like rabbits living in them.

Commentary

The narrator's fear is difficult to understand. Who is she afraid for, and what or whom is she afraid of? Up until this point we have assumed that she is afraid for her friends and herself, and is afraid of her father. Now we see that in addition to this, she also wants to protect her father from her friends and to save all of them from what she mysteriously refers to as "knowledge." Also, she hides the scrapbook she discovers in the bedroom because she doesn't want her friends "spying."

She doesn't trust her friends, and she doesn't trust her father. The reader begins to suspect that rather than protecting her friends, she is protecting herself. She doesn't want them to know anything about her father or herself.

Increasing evidence of the narrator's coldness emerges in this chapter. When Joe proposes to her, she has several reactions, all of them indicating a lack of feeling. First, she feels like laughing. Then she feels as if he's threatening her, wanting her to marry him even though she doesn't want to because her acceptance would please him. Even as she is telling him that she does care for him, she is planning to leave him and find a new apartment. Joe is becoming "three-dimensional," and this scares the narrator. As he becomes more of a complex person and less of a two-dimensional character whose reactions are predictable, she must take responsibility for the feelings she triggers in him. Previously, she never seemed to know what he was feeling and never asked. Now she knows; he is expressing his feelings too obviously to be ignored. She begins to respond in the robot-like manner she described in the previous chapter.

Her unusual memory of her wedding is like her earlier description of giving birth. Both seem to contain odd descriptions and both appear to refer to events other than a marriage or the birth of a baby.

Once again, the reader is alerted to the fact that the narrator's search for her father has also become a search for herself. As she looks through the scrapbooks, she is looking for something that will tell her where she had come from or gone wrong. She is looking for clues in the drawings and finds some in the pictures of Easter eggs. Away from violence or fear, the rabbits live in total safety but also in total isolation. The eggs have rope ladders that can be pulled up after them. She wonders if perhaps this "was a vision of Heaven." If it is a vision of Heaven, it is also a vision of alienation.

CHAPTER 11

Summary

After breakfast the next day, her father's friend, Paul, arrives. With him is a man named Bill Malmstrom, a member of the Detroit branch of the Wildlife Protection Association of America. He has "trimmed grey hair and an executive moustache like the shirt ads, the vodka ads; his clothes were woodsy, semi-worn, verging on the authentic." He and the rest of his branch want to buy the cabin to use as a retreat lodge, "where members could meditate and observe the beauties of nature. And maybe do a little hunting and fishing."

The narrator refuses his offer, saying that the cabin is not for sale. She feels that her father would be furious if he returned and found she'd sold his house. Feeling she should explain her position to Paul, she takes him into the garden and tells him that her father is still alive. When Paul asks if her father has returned, she says he's away on a trip, but will be back soon. She admits that she has not seen her father, but tells Paul that he left her a note, more or less.

When she tells her friends about Mr. Malmstrom, David is convinced that he is a CIA agent. His theory is that Americans are running out of clean water and are sending up spies to investigate Canada's supplies. He foresees the American government talking Canada into giving them water, an event that will be followed by an uprising by the "National Movement," a group of Canadian guerrillas. The narrator silently mocks his theory.

Later that evening, Anna expresses her anger over David's flirtations with the narrator. Although the narrator thought he was just teasing, Anna reveals that David often openly flirts with other women. Anna exposes her jealousy and David's frequent unfaithfulness. The narrator wishes Anna hadn't told her this because she wanted to believe that a good marriage had remained possible for somebody.

Commentary

Previously, the imagery that Atwood has used in her descriptions of alienation between people has been of a mechanical nature. The narrator's reduction of Joe into "an object in the bed, like a sack or a large turnip," is equally dehumanizing. It seems easier for the narrator to regard people as things than to try and deal with them as people with feelings.

Similarly, when Anna begins to tell the narrator about the truth behind her relationship with David, the narrator's reaction is that she wishes she hadn't been told. However, she doesn't wish this just because her myth of the ideal marriage is weakened, but also because Anna has revealed herself and her problems so intimately. The narrator does not want to know about

Anna's problems; she does not want to be responsible for her friend. Anna has told her these things partly to protect her from being mislead by David's flirtations, but the narrator would not have done the same for her.

From her conversation with Paul, it would seem that the narrator is certain her father is not dead. She leads him to believe that her father is on a trip and that he has left her a note telling her this. The narrator is making assumptions about her father's drawings, interpreting them very freely and believing what she wants to believe.

Although David has been portrayed as anti-American before, it is in this chapter that Atwood allows him to expose this part of his character more fully. His theories are so silly that Atwood's parody of reactionary nationalism becomes clear. A strong nationalist herself, Atwood is criticizing people who go too far and become narrow-minded and fanatical. She also attacks people like David who claim to be earnest in their beliefs but who actually do nothing to change things. David is a man of many words and few actions.

CHAPTER 12

Summary

The next day, while Anna and Joe are outside, David flirts with the narrator. She explains that she has to work and he leaves. Alone in the cabin, she doesn't work but begins to search for a will, deed or property title to the cottage. Since Paul seemed certain that her father was dead, she now doubts her theory about his hiding in the forest. She even suspects that the CIA had killed him to get the land. She searches unsuccessfully for any legal papers.

She suddenly remembers his drawings and decides to look through them more carefully. The first drawing she recognizes as a boat with people in it and she is pleased that she can make sense of it. She cannot make sense of the second drawing and decides that her father must have been totally mad. She decides that "the drawing was something he saw, a hallucination; or it might have been himself, what he thought he was turning into."

Just as she decides that her original thoughts were correct, she discovers a letter that proves her to be wrong. The letter is addressed to her father and thanks him for sending photographs, tracings and a map. Along with the letter is a copy of a recent article entitled "Rock Paintings of the Central Shield." Part of the article describes the paintings, comparing them to children's drawings. The author of the article attempts to explain what the drawings mean. He also offers theories of their function, one of which states that "the sites of the paintings are the abodes of powerful or protective spirits" and another that says that "the paintings are associated with the practice of fasting to produce significant or predictive dreams."

The narrator becomes upset at the realization that this letter explains the existence of the drawings and provides the solution to the mystery. Her father's drawings were part of a retirement hobby centered around rock paintings. She now has proof of his sanity and therefore of his probable death. He is not a madman lurking in the woods. Although she realizes she should feel either relief or grief, at this moment she feels only blank.

Two things are unsolved: the notes and the numbers on the drawings. She decides that they are a location code. After examining them, she finally spotted the key: a name she recognized, White Birch Lake, where she had been bass fishing. She finds it on a map, which has Xs all over it like a treasure map. She wants to verify the drawings and visit the location, deciding to disguise it as a fishing trip to her friends.

Anna enters the cabin and asks why Joe is so unhappy, and the narrator tells her about his proposal. The narrator realizes that not only does she not feel bad about it but she didn't feel much of anything, and hadn't for a long time. She wasn't always like this and thinks that "at some point my neck must have closed over, pond freezing or a wound, shutting me into my head." The narrator goes out to talk to Joe, who only wants to know if she loves him or not. She finds it difficult to answer, the problem "was the language again, I couldn't use it because it wasn't mine."

Later she gets the photo album out, thinking that it isn't her father's death that concerns her now but her own. She thinks that perhaps she would be able to tell when the change occurred by the difference in photos of herself. The pictures don't solve anything, though, they provide no hints or facts as to when the change had taken place. She decides that:

> I must have been all right then; but after that I'd allowed myself to be cut in two. Woman sawn apart in a wooden crate, wearing a bathing suit, smiling, a trick done with mirrors, I read it in a comic book; only with me there had been an accident and I came apart. The other half, the one locked away, was the only one that could live; I was the wrong half, detached, terminal. I was nothing but a head, or no, something minor like a severed thumb; numb. (p. 117)

Commentary

Paul's disbelief and the discovery of the letter finally convince the narrator her theory that her father is mad and hiding in the woods is wrong. She realizes that she created this secret; she has made a mystery where no mystery existed. Since her father's drawings were the only basis for her theory, the fact that the narrator has waited until now to take a closer look indicates her neglect in accepting this theory so readily. Once again, she had believed what she wanted to believe.

The pattern of the mystery story is evident in *Surfacing*, and this chapter is an important one in its development. Before, the narrator stopped looking for clues since she was convinced that her father was alive and should be left alone. She becomes the detective again, however, when she finds the letter and decides to solve the puzzle of the notes and numbers on the drawings. She realizes they indicate locations on a map that resembles a treasure map. Now she wants to verify the information by finding the paintings her father made the drawings of. As usual, she decides to keep her discovery from her friends and tells them they are going fishing.

The second mystery story also emerges in this chapter. This is the mystery of why the narrator doesn't appear to be able to experience emotions, why she envies Joe's obvious display of pain when she cannot say that she loves him. Significantly, she realizes that it is her own death that now concerns her, not just the death of her father. Like the detective in any mystery story, the narrator looks for clues to discover the circumstances surrounding the death, this time of herself. The photo album provides no evidence; she seemed to be all right as a young girl. She realizes, however, that at some point she became divided, her head became figuratively separated from her body. She can think, but she cannot feel. She is the "wrong half" of herself, the thinking half, and it is only the other half that can live. Life without feeling is a kind of death, and she must find the other half of herself so that she can begin living again.

CHAPTER 13

Summary

The next morning, Joe and the narrator discuss their situation. She offers to move out of the apartment when they get back to the city since all his pottery equipment is stored there. She continues to think that he sees the conflict as a contest he wants to win. As far as she is concerned, "he didn't love me, it was an idea of himself he loved and he wanted me to join him, anyone would do, I didn't matter so I didn't have to care."

They start out on the fishing trip in the canoes, stopping for lunch on an island that is littered with trash left by other campers. The narrator thinks back to the night before when she had wanted to be rescued. She thought that if her body had been made to respond strongly enough, some feeling might have made it through her "closed throat" into her head. She thinks about the concept of feelings, and she "rehearsed emotions, naming them: joy, peace, guilt, release, love and hate, react, relate; what to feel was like what to wear, you watched the others and memorized it. But the only thing there was the fear that I wasn't alive." She wants to be saved, to become alive again, but neither she nor Joe is willing to reconcile.

As they get into the canoes again and begin to paddle, her aching muscles tell her that at least her body was alive. Just before they reach the portage, they see some Americans going by in a powerboat. While they are on the portage she notices footprints. The prints head only one way, and she thinks that "whoever they were, Americans, maybe, spies, they were still in there." They reach the second portage and are confronted with a dead bird hanging upside down, tied by a thin blue nylon rope around its feet.

Commentary

The narrator's comments on Joe's response to her refusal of his proposal and their discussion of their relationship is revealing. First, she relishes the thought of being old because then she will presumably avoid such conflicts with men. She then refers to the conflict as a contest for Joe. She is convinced he doesn't love her and that any woman would do. Significantly, she neatly avoids responsibility for the situation by describing it this way and removes any possibility of guilt by arguing that "I didn't matter so I didn't have to care." Although we don't know much about the character of Joe, and what we do know we have seen through the narrator's eyes, it seems the situation is not as clear-cut as she would have us think. There is good reason to believe that Joe does love her, and that this is the reason he wants to marry her.

Interestingly, the narrator does realize that something is wrong with her inability to feel. She seems sincere in her desire to be cured and clearly sees Joe as a possible means of accomplishing this. She can rehearse emotions by naming them, but she cannot feel them. She merely watches what other people express and memorizes the emotions. Once again, she refers to her own symbolic death, the death of feeling. She is afraid that she isn't alive, and she isn't alive because her mind and her body are separated.

Her paranoia about her father following or threatening them is now replaced by a fear of Americans. She is suspicious of them, and when she discovers the footprints, she automatically thinks they belong to the Americans. She also suspects them of being spies. She finds the idea that they are still in the area very threatening.

CHAPTER 14

Summary

The dead bird is a heron. While David and Joe get the camera set up to take some shots of it, the narrator looks at the bird, disgusted that someone would kill it. Since it couldn't be eaten or tamed, it held no value for anyone except that it was beautiful to look at while it was still alive. The narrator thinks the only reason they killed and hung it was to destroy it, "to prove they could do it, they had the power to kill." Although she has no proof, she is certain that the Americans that they saw earlier are responsible.

They set off through the next portage. It is shorter but

more difficult than the other one because it is more thickly overgrown. She wonders what she will say to the Americans if they meet, but when they reach White Birch Lake there is no sign of them. They canoe towards a clearing and begin to set up camp, putting up tents and gathering firewood. While she is washing the dishes after dinner, the narrator sees the Americans' tent at the other end of the lake. She feels as if they are a threat.

They leave Anna at the campsite and go bass fishing in the canoe. David catches a fish and asks the narrator to kill it for him. She refuses. Suddenly she feels guilty about killing:

> I couldn't anymore. I had no right to. We didn't need it, our proper food was tin cans. We were committing this act, violation, for sport or amusement or pleasure, recreation they call it, these were no longer the right reasons. That's an explanation but no excuse my father used to say. (p. 129)

While David and Joe admire the fish the narrator releases the rest of the frogs into the water. She helps them put on other lures, but she still feels like she is taking part in a murder.

She spots the Americans coming towards them in a canoe. She assesses what she calls their disguises: "they weren't the bloated middle-aged kind, those would stick to powerboats and guides; they were younger, trimmer, with the candid, tanned astronaut finish valued by the magazines." They exchange fishing gossip as the narrator watches them carefully. According to her, they have "raygun fishing rods, faces impermeable as space-suit helmuts, sniper eyes." She is now convinced they killed the heron. She remembers stories she heard as a child about Americans:

> The ones who stuffed the pontoons of their seaplane with illegal fish, the ones who had a false bottom to their car, two hundred lake trout on dry ice . . . They got drunk and chased loons in their powerboats for fun, backtracking on the loon as it dived, not giving it a chance to fly, until it drowned or got chopped up in the propeller blades. Senseless killing, it was a game; after the war they'd been bored. (p. 130-131)

After they get back to the campsite, Anna tells the narrator that she has forgotten her makeup. Anna is extremely upset; she is sure David will get after her about it. She reveals sordid details about their marriage. David has a set of rules and if she breaks them, she is punished. When the narrator suggests a divorce, Anna explains that she loves him, even though she thinks he'd like her to die.

Joe appears to be asleep when the narrator enters the tent. He isn't asleep, and he says he wants them to return to the way their relationship was before. The narrator refuses, and Joe angrily turns away from her.

Commentary

Anger now joins the fear that the narrator directs towards the Americans. She is angry over the senseless killing of the heron and even more so by the way in which the body is displayed. Since there is no reason to kill a heron — it is not a threatening, dangerous animal, neither can it be eaten — she decides that they did it for the joy of killing something. She suspects that the Americans are responsible when she first sees the heron, and when they meet on the lake she is convinced.

The narrator feels guilty because she did not bury the bird. Her guilt plagues her, and when she closes her eyes, the shape of the heron haunts her. Similarly, she feels guilty about helping David and Joe catch fish. Even though she sets the frogs free, she is still an "accessory" to their other "murders." She has always been the one to kill the fish, but she suddenly feels as if she no longer has the right. Since they do not really need the fish as food, they are killing for recreation. This no longer seems to be a good reason for the narrator. Killing seems to be an activity done by Americans, and shouldn't be done by the narrator and her friends.

Her fear of the Americans grows. She suspects that they are watching her with binoculars, ready to shoot her. When she meets them, she thinks they have "sniper eyes." She even goes so far as to wish evil upon them. Although she seems to dislike violence, she wishes to see the "enemy" destroyed. Oddly enough, she does not confront them about the heron when she meets them, even though she is sure they killed it.

Finally, her description of Joe as "inert, comforting as a log" is very revealing. She wonders if "that was the only time there could be anything like love; when he was asleep, demanding nothing." She touches him as she would touch a tree or a stone. The narrator is only capable of loving an inanimate object. If the object is human, then it will make demands upon her. It will have feelings she may be responsible for. The narrator avoids such situations at all costs.

CHAPTER 15

Summary

The first to wake up the next day is the narrator. After cleaning the fish, she cooks breakfast for them. None of her friends are in a good mood: Anna and David didn't sleep well, and Joe had a nightmare. Anna looks particularly bad. Without her cream and makeup, her face is dry and shrivelled, and the narrator notices her wrinkles. David, however, doesn't seem to notice that anything is different.

The narrator buries the fish bones, thinking that some ways of killing things are more fair. If they had to dive for the fish and catch them with their teeth, the contest would be more natural. Instead of fishing, they set out to look for the rock paintings. David wants them in his film. They pass the Americans' campsite and don't see anyone. The narrator wonders if her evil wish worked, and they are dead.

Even by following the map, the narrator is unable to find the rock paintings, and she is angry. She feels as if her father has lied to her; she feels cheated. The others are also disappointed and they head back to their campsite.

They meet the Americans out in their canoe again, and the narrator thinks about the nature of killing. Her anger is still very strong, and she feels like she wants to hit the Americans with her paddle. The Americans ask them what state they're from and are surprised to hear that the narrator and her friends are Canadians. Ironically, the "Americans" turn out to be Canadians, too. The narrator is furious because she feels as if they've disguised themselves. In the end, she decides that it doesn't matter what country they're from. They killed the heron and acted like Americans. She is afraid that Canadians are turning into "Americans." She feels that "if you look like them and talk like them you are them, you speak their language."

Although David wants to stay and talk with the

"Americans," the narrator talks him out of it. She wants to get away from the "killers." As they pass the heron, the narrator feels guilty again. She feels "a sickening complicity, sticky as glue, blood on my hands, as though I had been there and watched without saying No or doing anything to stop it."

She recalls her brother used to catch crayfish, snakes and frogs and keep them in jars. She once set them free, and he never forgave her. After that, he caught more and hid them. Even though she eventually found them, she was too afraid to let them go and felt they were killed because of her reluctance. As a child, she "didn't want there to be wars and death, I wanted them not to exist; only rabbits with their coloured egg houses."

Commentary

When Joe has a nightmare that night, the narrator feels as if it's safe to touch him because he was in his sleeping bag. He is restrained; he can make no demands on her. She wakes him because she wants to know what he was dreaming about so that perhaps he could help her remember how. The narrator realizes that not dreaming is a bad thing.

Her confusion, guilt and anger about killing continues. She thinks about killing in an obsessive manner, examining all aspects of it. Some deaths are natural, like wolves killing old deer. Some deaths are fair, like catching fish in the water with your teeth. She has to justify every killing she experiences.

When the Americans turn out to be Canadians, the narrator still refers to them as "Americans" because she is convinced that they are killers. American has become for her not a nationality but a way of life, an attitude towards nature. "Americans" kill without justification, unfairly and unnaturally.

Her response as a child to killing was naive and passive. She didn't want there to be wars and death, she wanted everyone to be happy. This is obviously unrealistic, and now the narrator finds all killing difficult to accept. She wants to remove herself from anyone who kills anything. However, she realizes as they leave that "redemption was elsewhere, I must have overlooked it." She wants to be forgiven for being human, for being an accomplice. The clues her father offered her turn out to be misleading. Either he has lied to her, or she has misunderstood. She must now look elsewhere for her redemption.

CHAPTER 16

Summary

It is the sixth day. The narrator is getting anxious because Evans is coming tomorrow to pick them up, and she still hasn't found out what happened to her father or the correct location of the rock paintings. After she checks the map, she finds another marked site and decides to investigate it. The site she wants to check is underwater, so she will have to dive in order to see if the rock paintings are there.

As she goes down to the shore, she overhears an argument between David and Anna. Anna seems much happier now that the canoe trip is over, and she has fresh makeup on her face. At this moment, however, David is trying to talk her into taking her bathing suit off so that Joe can take some shots of her for the movie. He is trying to convince her verbally, and his voice has a "menacing gentleness" in it. The narrator wants to stop the fight but doesn't. She recalls that she used to fight when she was younger, but that after a while she no longer fought back because she never won.

Both Anna and David become very angry, and David threatens to throw her into the lake if she doesn't cooperate. She finally gives in, takes off her bathing suit and dives into the water while Joe films her.

The narrator walks down to get the canoe so that she can look for the rock paintings. Reflecting on what she has just seen, she thinks that David is like her: "we are the ones that don't know how to love, there is something missing in us." Joe and Anna, on the other hand, "are lucky, they do it badly and suffer because of it: but it's better to see than to be blind, even though that way you had to let in the crimes and atrocities too."

When the narrator asks David why he forced Anna to humiliate herself, he tells her that Anna is devious and unfaithful. Basically, David tells the narrator the same things about Anna that she had told the narrator about David. In addition to her unfaithfulness, Anna is, according to David, stupid.

Remembering what Anna had told her about the necessity of emotional commitments, the narrator suddenly realizes that Anna and David's commitment is not based on mutual love and respect: "they hate each other; that must be almost as absorbing as love." She realizes that they will not forgive each other or mention the incident since they are somehow beyond that. As far as the narrator can tell, they had reached a balance in life somewhat like peace.

She leaves all of them behind at the cabin as she gets into the canoe and sets off to try and find the rock paintings.

Commentary

Once again, the narrator is acting like a detective, determined to solve the mystery of her father's disappearance. She is getting better at her detective work, however, searching for clues and following leads more carefully. Instead of giving up when she can't find the first rock painting, she checks the map again and decides to try and find another one. The search now has a tone of urgency since she has only one day left to solve the mystery.

Her refusal to take part in the argument between Anna and David points to her avoidance of involvement. Although she wants to try and stop the fight, she doesn't do anything. She doesn't want to become involved in anyone else's problems, and the best way to achieve this is simply to pretend you haven't noticed anything. Her answer to the tension between her and Joe is, for example, that she move out of their apartment.

Significantly, she realizes that, like David, something is missing in her: the ability to love. Joe and Anna have this quality. The narrator comes to realize that even though they will suffer and will have to put up with cruelty, it is better to see how things are than to be blind. Both she and David are blind. They refuse to acknowledge anyone else's pain. They refuse to accept responsibility for anyone else's feelings.

When the narrator tries to convince David that Anna loves him, she realizes that "it was the magic word but it couldn't work because I had no faith." Once again, language becomes meaningless. The word "love" has lost its significance for her because her husband used to repeat it over and over again. Language is insufficient for David as well. Ironically, even though he teaches a course in "Communications," there is no real communication between himself and his wife. As with the narrator, the word "love" has lost its meaning. It comes as a shock to the narrator when she finally sees that her concept of the ideal marriage, the barometer couple in Paul's house, is not really ideal: "they were glued there, condemned to oscillate back and forth, sun and rain, without escape." The barometer couple, like David and Anna, are joined together, but they are not joined together by love.

CHAPTER 17

Summary

As the narrator paddles the canoe towards the cliff where she thinks the rock painting is, she remembers the herons she has seen. A plane flying overhead reminds her of the first heron they saw. The dead heron they discovered resembles Christ: "whether it died willingly, consented, whether Christ died willingly, anything that suffers and dies instead of us is Christ." The idea of killing animals, whether their flesh is eaten or not, suddenly becomes horrible to her because it is not done with any respect or religious feeling.

She reaches the cliff and she prepares to dive. On her first dive, she moves along the cliff underwater but doesn't find anything. After waiting for a few moments and moving the canoe further along, she dives again. She doesn't find anything this time either but is still convinced something was there. Her father would not have marked and numbered the map so carefully for nothing.

She dives again and thinks she sees something, a blotch or a shadow. After resting, she dives a fourth time, deeper into the darkness of the lake. This time she does see something:

> It was there but it wasn't a painting, it wasn't on the rock. It was below me, drifting towards me from the furthest level where there was no life, a dark oval trailing limbs. It was blurred but it had eyes, they were open, it was something I knew about, a dead thing, it was dead. (p. 152)

She is terrified and swims towards the canoe, discovering when she gets there that Joe has arrived in the other canoe. She reaches the canoe in a state of complete panic and climbs in.

Lying on the bottom of the canoe, she trys to figure out what she has seen: "at first I thought it was my drowned brother, hair floating around the face, image I'd kept from before I was born; but it couldn't be him." She then recognizes that "it wasn't even my brother I'd been remembering, that was a disguise." She then thinks of what she saw as if it had been in a bottle, and she recalls a traumatic abortion she has had.

She recalls knocking the bottle off a table and breaking it, before realizing that had never happened. What did happen was that she went to a shabby house, had an abortion, and was picked up by her boyfriend afterwards. She couldn't accept such a traumatic experience and created a different one to ease her guilt.

It was after the abortion that she decided she could never go home again. She was convinced that her parents wouldn't be able to understand the "evil" she had done. Her boyfriend had told her that the fetus wasn't a person, that it was only an animal. The narrator realizes that she is responsible for its death, that she was as much of a killer as those who performed the abortion. After the abortion, which she calls a "murder," she refuses to see her boyfriend again and carries the guilt of the abortion with her.

The narrator now believes that her father's maps and drawings mean something different. At first they may have been part of a hobby, but then he had found out that "the Indians did not own salvation but they had once known where it had lived and their signs marked the sacred places, the places where you could learn the truth." The new places that he had discovered were ones where he saw things the way the narrator has just seen something: "true vision, at the end, after the failure of logic." The maps indicate sacred places where a person could experience such a vision.

The narrator feels like making an offering to the Indian gods so she places her sweatshirt on a ledge near the cliff. She feels as if she has received a gift from them. Joe follows her and attempts to make love to her. The narrator suddenly feels as if sex would be a sacrilegious experience, and she refuses him, explaining that she is afraid of becoming pregnant.

Commentary

This is the most crucial and the most confusing chapter in *Surfacing*. It is important that the reader examine it very closely. This is the turning point in the story: the plot has been moving in one direction and suddenly it changes and begins to move in another direction.

The realization that the narrator has had an abortion is a shock to us because we suddenly recognize we have been lied to by the narrator. She has told us, on several occasions, that she was married, had a child and left the child with her husband when they divorced.

The last time she dives, she encounters something in the water. We are not sure if it is a real object or a vision, but for her it represents the child that she did not have. At first, she mistakes it for her brother, but this is a "disguise." Her memories of the wedding and the birth of her child have also been disguises. She was not able to accept what she had done, or allowed to be done to her, and created false memories.

We learn that she did not have the abortion in a hospital but in a house. The man she has been referring to as her husband was actually her boyfriend. A married man, he wasn't even able to take her to the house since his children were having a birthday party that day.

The narrator's obsession with killers, hunters and fishermen gains new meaning as she comes to the realization that "I could have said no to the abortion, but I didn't; that made me one of them too, a killer." She has been lying to others, including the reader, and to herself because she wanted to escape the moral responsibility for the death of her child. It was easier for the narrator to present herself as the victim of a broken marriage because that would not have been entirely her fault.

Like any good mystery novel, the reader was given hints that suggested her marriage and child were make-believe. When we look back to the description of her marriage, we recall the odd use of the word "antiseptic." Her description of giving birth now makes more sense since we realize it is actually a description of an abortion. The fountain is the subtlest clue. We see it as the narrator and her friends are driving north, in her description of her wedding and in her description of the abortion.

This chapter is also important because it highlights the development of the religious quest in *Surfacing*. Now that the narrator sees the truth of her past, she must try and reconcile what she has done with what she has come to believe about killing. She suggests at the beginning of the chapter that there is a sacramental relationship between humans and nature that humans choose to ignore. She recognizes that the map refers to sacred places where Indians once had religious or mystic experiences. She requires salvation, and the gods have provided her with a vision that forces her to see the reality of her past. These same gods give her another gift, since the narrator senses that feeling was beginning to creep back into her. Her awareness of the religious aspect of her experience is clear when she makes an offering of her shirt to the gods and when she refuses Joe's advances.

Thus the narrator clearly sees this experience as a religious one: she has been granted a vision of the truth, and she has been given back her sense of feeling by the ancient Indian gods. The experience may also be interpreted as a psychological one. The narrator has dived into the depths of her unconscious and has confronted what she had hidden there because of her intense feelings of guilt. After confronting and accepting the truth about what she has done, she is beginning to get well. She is beginning to experience emotions again.

CHAPTER 18

Summary

The narrator returns to the cabin and sits on the swing she used to play on as a child. Looking at the wedding ring she still wears triggers memories of her former lover. She recalls that the ring was used to make it easier for them to get motel rooms.

Hearing a powerboat motor, she watches what she thinks are Americans going by in a boat. She feels as if they are surveying, planning an attack and a takeover. When they head towards the cliff where she was diving, she feels as if it's dangerous for them since they don't know about the power that is there. She was safe only because her father's maps and drawings protected her like a lucky talisman.

David comes by and to avoid talking to him, the narrator goes for a walk in the bush. While she is thinking about language and the human desire to name things, she discovers that David has followed her. He interrupts her thoughts, and she has trouble talking to him because: "the English words seemed imported, foreign." He thinks she wanted him to follow her and tries to convince her to make love to him. When she refuses, he becomes angry and tells her that Joe is with Anna. He argues that it would be a good form of revenge or justice if he and the narrator made love. She refuses once again and returns to the cabin.

The narrator regards her father's maps and drawings as a gift to her, and now she wants to find her mother's gift, which she thinks is hidden in the cabin. Her father's gift gave only knowledge. She is convinced that her mother's gift will show her not only how to see, but how to act.

Later, when the four of them are sitting around the table, David implies that he made love to the narrator, and she denies it. Both Anna and David taunt her, calling her a man-hater.

Commentary

When the narrator returns to the cabin after her experiences underwater, she is changed. That part of her that seemed to be missing has begun to return, and she is seeing things in a different way.

As she thinks about her former lover, she seems to dwell on the most humiliating and most painful moments. Now she is beginning to face the truth about him. At the time she worshipped him and later she lied to herself and to others and pretended he was her husband. At neither point did she see him as he was: an older man who was having an affair with a young woman, a man who was willing to risk nothing and expected everything in return.

Ironically, her father's drawings and maps that were once a source of confusion and embarrassment are now regarded as a gift. She feels as if her father left her these things as a kind of inheritance, a way of helping her become well. Her father's gift was knowledge: it taught her how to see the truth. Her mother's gift, when she finds it, will teach her how to act.

The power that she feels she has gotten in touch with seems to be the strength to see things as they really are. The journey to the power was frightening and dangerous, but she can now face reality, even if it is cruel and difficult to accept.

The narrator's concern with language continues in this chapter, and the power also seems to help her see things without the intrusion of words. When she is walking in the woods, her way of looking at things is different: "sight flowing ahead of me over the ground, eyes filtering the shapes, the names of things fading but their forms and uses remaining." She is learning to see as an animal sees. More and more, she feels herself alienated from the English language. She has difficulty understanding what David is saying to her when he meets her in the woods. It seems necessary for her to try and deal with the world without language. As she thinks to herself when Joe wants to make love to her, "language divides us into fragments, I wanted to be whole."

CHAPTER 19

Summary

Before supper, the narrator searches the toolshed for her mother's gift but doesn't find anything. She is sure she will recognize it because it will be something that is out of place. She looks for clues everywhere, even examining the dishes to make sure none of them are different. After supper she searches in her bedroom, and as soon as she steps inside she feels the "power," she feels as if she's close to the gift. Suddenly she realizes that it must be in the scrapbooks she'd discovered earlier since they weren't supposed to be there, they belonged in the city.

While she's searching, a powerboat arrives and David and Anna come back to the cabin to tell her that her father has been found by some American fishermen. His body was unrecognizable, but Paul identified the clothes as her father's. The narrator is suspicious of the information, and when she asks them where they found the body, they tell her that it was near the cliff where she was diving. The narrator doesn't believe them. Nevertheless, she plays along and pretends to believe them. She has read enough murder mysteries to know what to invent.

She returns to the bedroom to look at the scrapbooks, and one feels heavier and warmer. Letting it fall open, she sees her mother's gift. The gift is a drawing that the narrator did as a child of a woman with a round moon stomach. A baby was sitting up inside her gazing out. She feels that the picture is her guide. Her mother had saved it for her, and now she had to try and understand its new meaning with the help of the "power."

As the boat leaves and her friends return to the cabin and begin to play cards, the narrator feels that David and Anna are becoming machines. For Joe, however, "truth might still be possible, what will preserve him is the absence of words." As for herself, she feels she has to "immerse myself in the other language'' before she can totally understand her mother's gift. Even though her friends are avoiding her because of the news of her father's death, the narrator is convinced that ''nothing has died, everything is alive, everything is waiting to become alive.''

Commentary

The quest for her mother's gift has begun to be an obsession with the narrator. The mystery of her father's death seems to be unimportant. When her friends tell her that his body has been found, her reaction is very strange. Instead of feeling grief or even relief that the mystery is finally solved, she feels suspicion. She is convinced they are lying and the report of his death is a trap designed to hurt her. When the reader hears the body was discovered where the narrator was diving, however, it becomes clear that the ''dead thing'' the narrator saw underwater was the body of her father. This does not seem important to the narrator. What is important now is the quest for meaning, and the discovery of her mother's gift is a crucial step in that quest.

The drawings she discovers are of a pregnant woman and a man with horns on his head and a barbed tail. Although these pictures originally represented God and the Devil, the narrator must now reinterpret them. Significantly, she has already described her father's gift of knowledge by saying that ''his gods were of the head, antlers rooted in the brain.'' It is, therefore, the pregnant woman who represents her mother's gift: how to act.

PART THREE • CHAPTER 20

Summary

Later that same night, the narrator waits in the bedroom, listening to the sounds of her friends getting ready to go to bed. When Joe enters the room, she senses that he is uneasy. After the encounter with Anna and the news of the narrator's father, Joe isn't sure how to approach her. He thinks she must be in pain and tries not to wake her up. The narrator reaches out to hold him, but his skin smells not only of Anna's suntan lotion but of civilization: the sheets, wool and soap.

She leads him outside. He has trouble walking in the dark, but the narrator is able to lead them both. They make love outside, and the narrator says she can feel her lost child surfacing. She is determined to deliver this child herself and is also determined that she will never teach it any words. She will give birth to it like an animal and raise it like an animal.

She doesn't tell Joe that she suspects she is pregnant, while he tells her that his encounter that afternoon with Anna was meaningless. He wants to know if she loves him, but she doesn't answer.

Commentary

Like the beginning of Part Two, the beginning of Part Three is marked by a change in tense. Atwood now returns to the use of the present tense, and this change signals a change in plot and characterization. The narrator has explored and confronted her past in Part Two, which was narrated in the past tense. Now she is ready to confront and explore the present.

Throughout this chapter, the narrator makes several references to animals and humans. When Joe enters the bedroom and takes off his clothes, she says that he "unzips his human skin." Similarly, it is not the smells that remind her of Anna that repel her, but the smells of civilization on Joe's skin. She doesn't want to make love inside but instead outside where animals would mate. She has previously described Joe as if he were an animal, but now she realizes that "he needs to grow more fur." The narrator, on the other hand, seems to be growing more and more animal-like. She appears to be able to see in the dark and describes herself as having tentacled feet.

She wants to act like an animal because she feels that is the natural way to act. To act like an animal is to regain a sense of harmony with nature. As they are making love, she feels she is pregnant, even though she could not yet be sure of this. Significantly, she senses that her aborted child is surfacing within her, forgiving her for having killed it. The narrator has seen and confronted her guilt about the abortion. Now she is acting to make amends for her wrongdoing. Becoming pregnant again is an act of redemption; she will be forgiven for having killed a child if she brings another into the world. Becoming pregnant is the natural fulfilment of her mother's gift, the picture of the pregnant woman. The narrator has learned how to act.

CHAPTER 21

Summary

It is the morning of the next day, and the narrator is the last to wake up. Anna is already making breakfast in the kitchen, and everyone seems to be sure that the narrator and Joe's relationship has been saved. After breakfast, they pack and carry their luggage down to the dock to wait for Evans to pick them up.

Anna is dressed in her "urban costume" of bellbottoms and makeup. The narrator is uneasy about Anna's obsession with her appearance. She feels that everything that Anna does or wears is an imitation of something else.

David is discussing their film and Anna reminds him that they have film of her but none of the narrator. The narrator regards the film as a threat. She feels it is partially responsible for Anna's unnaturalness. While David and Joe carry one of the canoes up to the shed, the narrator takes the cannisters of film out of the camera bag and unravels them into the lake, destroying them. Anna is shocked, but she doesn't interfere.

The narrator sees Joe and David coming back for the other canoe and jumps into it, paddling out into the lake as David discovers his destroyed film. While her friends on shore are in a state of confusion, for the narrator "the direction is clear. I can see I've been planning this, for how long I can't tell."

She lies down in the canoe to wait and falls asleep. The sound of a motor wakes her up, and she beaches the canoe and goes into the woods where she can watch the others get in to Evans' boat. Before they leave, Anna and Joe call out the narrator's name, but she doesn't answer. As far as she is concerned, "I no longer have a name. I tried for all those years to be civilized but I'm not and I'm through pretending." After they leave, the narrator realizes how crazy she must now seem to other people.

Commentary

Anna's dependency upon makeup has always puzzled the narrator. She found it hard to believe that Anna would be so afraid of being seen without it. Now the narrator sees the makeup as representing far more than just Anna's attempts to please her husband. She regards it as a mask, something that disguises the real person behind the makeup. For the narrator, makeup is only part of a process that traps women into pretending to feel and be what they are not. It is the ultimate example of unnatural behaviour because women use it to imitate others.

Similarly, the narrator regards David and Joe's film as a trap. Just as Anna's true self is imprisoned behind a mask of makeup, so she is also imprisoned in the reels of film. When the narrator unravels the reels into the lake, she imagines the captured images swimming away.

The idea that the narrator is on a personal quest for meaning is evident in her statement that "the direction is clear. I see I've been planning this." She is not only escaping from her friends but is beginning to search for something. She now regards her friends as threats to this quest.

The narrator is beginning to go through several changes. Convinced she is pregnant, she feels her body changing. More and more, she is beginning to function like an animal. She feels she doesn't have a name anymore; language seems meaningless.

CHAPTER 22

Summary

The narrator returns to the cabin and discovers that they have locked it. She imagines that they think she has run away. She breaks a window and manages to get into the cabin. Once inside, she doesn't know what to do next so she unpacks and leafs through a magazine.

The power that she seemed to have received when she dived

into the lake is gone. She feels as if she is empty and ordinary again. Because she can think of nothing else to do, she goes to sleep.

She wakes up hungry and decides to get some food from the garden. Once she gets there, however, she starts crying. She does not feel that she is mourning for her parents. She is crying because she is angry with them for leaving her. She calls out that she is there, hoping that they will appear. Finally, she decides that she should will them back and then begins to sense the presence of her parents hiding out of sight in the woods.

After cooking her supper, she walks towards the outhouse, panicking when she is inside. Afraid, she runs back to the cabin and once inside she replaces the broken window. She feels as if the "power" would have protected her, but it has not yet returned to her.

As she prepares to go to sleep, she wonders if her friends will return and plans how she will escape if they do. Fear returns when she wakes up in the middle of the night. She senses that her parents want to get inside the cabin, but she is afraid to let them in. She realizes that they won't be who they once were. Although she has willed them back, she is terrified now that she feels they have returned.

Commentary

The narrator has begun a quest for something. She says that it is the "truth" that she has remained behind to find. But she is looking for not only the truth about the death of her father — indeed, this seems to be the last thing on her mind — but also the truth about herself. When she begins to cry and realizes that she is furious with her parents, the reader recognizes that the narrator is finally reacting emotionally to things. Her feelings have begun to return, and she is on her way to becoming whole again.

Her quest for truth is connected with what she calls the "power." Although this power is not clearly defined, it seems to be a combination of the force of nature and the ancient Indian gods that she became aware of and in touch with after she dived into the lake. Psychologically, it could also be seen as the power of the unconscious. All of these powers are dangerous, and when the narrator wakes up in the middle of the night, she is scared. Her quest is dangerous, difficult and confusing. She feels that the power has left her and without it, she is without protection or directions. She knows she must remain, but she is unsure what her next step should be.

CHAPTER 23

Summary

After waking up the next morning and having breakfast, the narrator begins to brush her hair. Suddenly, she feels a surge of fear and realizes that the power is present again, but in a different form. She recognizes that there are certain rules she must now follow: using a brush or looking in a mirror is now forbidden. She turns the mirror to the wall.

The power has returned and now her parents' presence offers her direction. As she leaves the cabin, she feels the fear leave as well. She realizes that there are places she's allowed to be in, other places she's not. Two places that are forbidden are the enclosure with the swing and the sandpile. Approaching the dock, she senses she is allowed near the water but not on the dock.

She then senses what her parents want her to do and returns to the cabin, building a fire in the woodstove. She burns her drawings and the typescript, and destroys her briefcase. The ring her former lover gave her is purified by dropping it into the fire, and "everything from history" is then burnt: the scrapbooks, her father's maps and drawings and the photo album. She then destroys the glasses, plates, books, blankets and clothes. When nothing is left, she leaves, taking one of the ripped blankets with her.

Walking to the lake, she lies down in the water and removes her clothes, letting them float away. Although she's hungry, she senses that the food in the cabin is now forbidden, as is the cabin itself. Wrapped in her blanket, she gathers some vegetables from the garden and eats them. She makes herself a place to sleep near the woodpile and falls asleep.

Commentary

The narrator's quest has now begun to take a more definite shape. With the return of the power, she knows what she is supposed to do. When she is doing something forbidden, fear tells her that it is wrong. She feels not only that there are rules she must follow, but also that there are certain things that she must do, certain rituals to be performed. The power seems to come not only from nature, but from what she perceives as the presence of her parents. She wants to make contact in some way with them: "It is time that separates us, I was a coward, I would not let them into my age, my place. Now I must enter theirs." She understands now that rituals must be performed in a certain order if her quest is to be successful.

One of the first rituals is that she must burn everything connected to civilization: drawings, photographs and maps. The burning of these things and the destruction of those things that can't be burned is a purging ritual; the fire purifies impure things. The next ritual she performs is just as ancient: she baptizes herself in the water. Like fire, water has long been used as a symbolic means of removing impurities. The individual who is baptized is symbolically born again. Most important, a baptism purifies and cleanses a person. In order to undertake the other rituals necessary to complete her quest, the narrator must be purified. Ever since her dive in the lake, her first baptism, the narrator has been involved in a process of atonement and rebirth. Her quest is clearly a visionary one, and she must search for the power of the gods, the ancient Indian gods of nature, through a ritual of personal purification.

CHAPTER 24

Summary

When the narrator wakes up the next morning, she is hungry. She runs towards the garden but stops when she reaches the gate. She realizes the garden is now forbidden. Wondering about the garden, she suddenly feels as if she understands the rule: "they can't be anywhere that's marked out, enclosed . . . they are against borders." She realizes that if she wants to make contact with the presence of her parents, she must be in the same condition they are in.

The narrator begins to search for food in the woods, gathering and eating edible plants and mushrooms. As she thinks about her future child, she suddenly feels sick and dizzy, with extreme pain in her stomach.

She retraces the trail and begins to notice that something is happening to her: her eyesight is altered and she feels like she is floating above the ground. She sees the forest as it was before the lumber company cut the trees, and everything she sees seems to melt, "everything is made of water, even the rocks." As she leans against a tree, she feels as if she is also a leaning tree.

After a while, she stands up and walks towards the cabin. Watching the birds, she suddenly sees her mother the way she must have looked shortly before the narrator was born. As she watches, the narrator is afraid her mother will vanish and suddenly, she does.

Commentary

As the narrator's visionary quest proceeds, she becomes aware of more rules. However, when she senses that she cannot enter the garden, she also comes to understand why. Her parents, in whatever form they exist, cannot enter areas that are enclosed. The narrator realizes that if she is to make contact with them, she must become as close as possible to whatever they are.

After she feels dizzy and sick, she experiences a vision. The visionary experience is one of total harmony with nature. She experiences a disintegration of herself and an integration with nature. When she leans against the tree, she becomes the tree. Nature is no longer something she is alienated from or afraid of. She is now part of nature.

Because she has followed the rules and performed the prescribed rituals, she is rewarded with another vision: that of her mother. This is also a vision of total harmony with nature since, when she vanishes, the narrator feels that her mother has been transformed into a bird.

CHAPTER 25

Summary

The narrator is awoken suddenly the next day by the sound of a powerboat. She sees it as a threat and runs into the woods to hide. She thinks it might be the police or possibly tourists. She even wonders if the war has started, and they are American invaders. She is afraid they will shoot her and hang her upside down in a tree like the dead heron. As they land, she can smell the scent of civilization on them "stale air, bus stations and nicotine smoke, mouths lined with soiled plush, acid taste of copper wiring or money."

She doesn't understand the words they are speaking, but as she listens she suddenly laughs. The five men, one of whom is Joe, hear her and begin chasing her as she runs through the woods and hides. Eventually, they give up the search and leave. As she walks back towards the cabin, she senses a new rule: she is forbidden to walk on the paths.

Suddenly the narrator sees her father standing with his back to her. As she calls him, however, she realizes that it is not her father, "it is what my father has become." Moments later, she sees a fish jump and recognizes that her father has been transformed into a fish. Returning to the fence where she saw him standing, she sees some footprints. Placing her feet in them, she discovers that they are her own.

Commentary

The narrator feels that the people approaching in the boat are a threat. She is afraid that she will be killed and hung like the heron she saw on the portage. It is difficult for her to understand them. She first mistakes their clothes for their skin. She can hear them speaking, but she can't tell if it's English or French: "I don't recognize it as any language I've ever heard or known." She is now beyond language. She is too close to nature to understand the communication of civilization.

Like her mother, her father appears to her in a vision. In the same way that she witnessed her mother transforming into a bird, she sees her father change into a fish. Both her parents have become embodiments of nature, taking on the shapes of animals. The end of the vision is signalled when the fish her father was transformed into becomes an ordinary fish again. The end of her visionary quest is marked by her stepping into what she expected to be her father's footprints, discovering that they are her own.

CHAPTER 26

Summary

Later that evening, the narrator makes herself another place to sleep and after eating nothing, falls asleep. During the night, she dreams about her parents and the way they were when they were still alive. When she wakes up the next morning, she realizes "they have gone finally, back into the earth, the air, the water, wherever they were when I summoned them." She also realizes that the time of rules is gone. She is now free to go back into all the places that had been forbidden. Even though she isn't hungry, she enters the cabin to get some food and is shocked to see the way she had destroyed things inside.

She thinks back to her first lover, but now remembers him more clearly and compassionately and feels only sorrow. She realizes that he was neither as ideal nor as cruel as she had thought, he "was only a normal man, middle-aged, second-rate, selfish and kind in the average proportions."

Autumn is not far off, and soon it will be winter. The narrator realizes she can't stay there forever. She wonders now if the people in the powerboat had come not to hurt her, but to warn her that she wouldn't be able to survive. She decides that she could paddle the canoe back to the village the next day and get back to the city from there.

The narrator now recognizes that her parents, whom she had perceived as "gods," have now gone and she begins to appreciate them as they were when they were alive. Turning the mirror around to look at herself, she realizes that she looks odd, wrapped only in a dirty blanket.

Commentary

The narrator's visionary experience is now over. She senses that the rules are gone, but so is her ability to experience visions, such as those of her parents. She now realizes that her parents will never appear to her again. Most importantly, she realizes that she will have to go on living. She eats even though she is not hungry because it is her duty to her parents and to herself as a human being to prefer life over death.

The narrator has changed in a number of important ways. She has had a dream during the night, and dreaming was one of the things she had not been able to do for some time. She begins to see others for what they really are and realizes how she used to distort things and people, imagining them to be whatever she wanted. She recalls her "husband" as being only normal, not the prince she thought he was when she was young and not the beast she thought he was when she was older. She also begins to see her parents more realistically. When she tries to picture them, "they dwindle, grow, become what they were, human. Something I never gave them credit for." She grows more sympathetic and wonders what their lives had actually been like.

CHAPTER 27

Summary

The narrator makes an important decision: to refuse to be a victim. She realizes that she has to stop thinking she is powerless and can therefore hurt no one. It is no longer possible to withdraw from people, and she gets ready to re-enter life by putting her clothes on.

She wonders about the baby she is carrying. If she is pregnant, she feels it is her duty to feed and take care of herself so that it will be a healthy baby.

She sees a boat arrive with Paul and Joe in it and goes into the woods. Joe gets out of the boat and he calls for her. She realizes that he must have stayed behind when David and Anna left and that he has returned for her.

Thinking about the possibility of her future relationship with Joe, she realizes that things will not always be easy. They will not be able to return to the way they were before, always avoiding each other and therefore avoiding any conflict between them. They must begin again. She is cautious, but she thinks she trusts Joe and might return with him to the city.

Commentary

In this final chapter, we see more evidence of the ways in which the narrator has changed as a result of her recent experiences. She realizes that in the past she has avoided taking responsibility for her actions by pretending that she was powerless and could not hurt anyone. By accepting the truth about her past, especially about her abortion, she has also come to accept responsibility for herself and her actions. She is not a passive victim; she is just as capable of hurting someone as anyone else. As long as she pretended that she was the victim of a failed marriage, for example, she could avoid taking responsibility for her love affair and the abortion she had as a result. Running away and distorting the truth is no longer a way of dealing with herself and others.

When Joe arrives, the narrator sees him as "a mediator, an

ambassador.'' He seems to stand midway between the natural world and the civilized world. Although she seems uncertain about whether to return to the city with him, we suspect that she will. She realizes that although their relationship won't be perfect, it has a good chance. She recognizes their past problems and knows that they will have to stop avoiding each other and begin to try and talk. Language, one of the central things she left behind during her visionary experience, is imperfect, but it is the only way to try and understand how another person is feeling.

The ending is uncertain, and there is no way of telling what the narrator will actually do. The ending is also full of hope, however, hope that is based on what seem to be realistic expectations and an acceptance that life is not perfect.

Character Sketches

Narrator

As the central character of the novel, the narrator is the one person we know the most about. In contrast, many of the secondary characters in *Surfacing* are two-dimensional or flat. Most of what we know of them is limited to how the narrator feels like describing them. The narrator, on the other hand, is provided with a fuller background, which helps to explain certain things in her personality and behaviour. In addition, she is revealed to us both by what she says and by what she doesn't say.

The character that the narrator's voice establishes at the beginning of the book seems to be a certain type of contemporary woman: cool, uninvolved and unemotional. We soon learn that this coolness masks a feeling of alienation from others. The narrator is not simply unemotional but is full of repressed emotion and, as a result, full of tension and anxiousness.

As the narrator journeys north to the family cabin where her father has been living, the reader begins to see that she, like her friends, is completely cut off from her past. She stopped visiting her parents several years ago, seeing her mother only briefly before she died and having no contact at all with her father. The fact that the narrator remains nameless also reinforces the idea that she is cut off from her past and her true identity.

Looking at the narrator's background, we slowly see some of the reasons for her alienation and her inability to feel. Her relationship with her parents has never been close. Although her father talked with her when she was young, his conversation was usually about concepts of reason and did not draw the two together. Her mother, on the other hand, did not seem to speak much at all. Although the narrator and her brother played together, his attraction to violence began to separate them.

Forced to divide her time between the anonymity of large cities and the isolation of the island, the narrator's alienation increases as she grows older. She is awkward and shy with other school children, and they tease and torment her. As she grows older, she begins to imitate the behaviour of others and does not say or do what she really feels. She abandons her dream of becoming an artist, for example, because her teacher tells her there have never been any famous woman artists. As a commercial artist, she draws whatever will please her publisher. In addition, her relationship with Joe reveals that she is not simply aloof but is empty of any emotions. She recalls that he was impressed by her coolness the first time they made love. The narrator, however, did not find her behaviour unusual because she *really* didn't feel anything.

When the truth of the narrator's early love affair and abortion are revealed, the reader suddenly learns a great deal more about her personality. Unable to accept the truth about her past, she began cutting herself off from her feelings because of the pain and guilt she was experiencing. She constructed elaborate, false stories to lessen her pain. Once she comes face to face with the truth, she allows herself to experience that pain and begins to unlock her feelings. By accepting her past the way it really was, she also accepts the guilt and responsibility that goes with it. By the end of the novel, she is a more emotional and less alienated person. She is less suspicious of others and begins to see Joe's wish to marry her as an expression of love and not as an attempt to overcome and conquer her.

Joe

Although Joe is only a secondary character, the reader gets to know more about him than Anna or David. The narrator's early descriptions of him are brief and two-dimensional, but his personality grows as her awareness of him as a person grows.

A professional potter, Joe is, in the eyes of the narrator and most people, a failure. Although he makes large, difficult pots with a great deal of skill, he then distorts their shapes by bending them. Forced to teach pottery to "aspiring housewives," he sells very little of his work in handicraft shops.

Like the narrator, Joe is an alienated and anxious person. He has nightmares that portray him as if he were a frightened child:

> He woke me when it was still dark, sitting up and saying "Where is this?" Every time we're in a new place he does that. "It's all right," I said, "I'm here," and though he said "Who? Who?", repeating it like an owl, he allowed me to ease him back down

> into bed. I'm afraid to touch him at these times, he might mistake me for one of the enemies in his nightmare. (p. 45)

It is not just the narrator he is alienated from, but everyone he meets. He says almost nothing to David and Anna. When he and David are working on their film, he usually just runs the camera and does not involve himself in the decision-making.

The narrator's use of metaphors, comparing Joe to the buffalo on the U.S. nickel, implies that Joe has more in common with an animal than he does with humans. The narrator says that, although he's moody and his temperment "alternates between surliness and gloom," he doesn't talk very much and "everything I value about him seems to be physical."

Because, as the narrator puts it, "speech to him was a task, a battle, words mustered behind his beard and issued forth one at a time, heavy and square like tanks," Joe increases his alienation from people by not expressing what he feels in words. The narrator and her friends can only guess what his feelings are.

Yet Joe is an emotional man. As the narrator notes, he is able to love people, and he suffers as a result. When he proposes to the narrator, expressing his feelings out loud, she suddenly sees him "growing larger, becoming alien, three-dimensional." As his unhappiness and anger at her refusal of his proposal are revealed, both the narrator and the reader recognize that his silence masked a sensitive man and not just a dumb animal in a man's clothing.

Anna

Although Anna is the narrator's best friend, most of what we learn of her is either negative or sad. The narrator does not know Anna very well, and her first impressions of her are that she is a well-adjusted woman with a good marriage. Anna is soon revealed to be a pathetic person, dependent upon cosmetics and a sadistic husband.

The narrator is shocked to see Anna in the kitchen early one morning putting on her makeup, and she realizes that "I've never seen her without it before, shorn of the pink cheeks and heightened eyes her face is curiously battered, a worn doll's." Anna claims that David doesn't know she wears makeup and is frantic when she discovers that she has forgotten to bring it on the fishing trip. Anna seems trapped in an image that others — especially David — have of her, and she seems to ask for the destruction of her personality that results:

> Rump on a packsack, harem cushion, pink on the cheeks and black discreetly around the eyes, as red as blood as black as ebony, a seamed and folded imitation of a magazine picture that is itself an imitation of a woman who is also an imitation, the original nowhere, hairless lobed angel in the same heaven where God is a circle, captive princess in someone's head. She is locked in, she isn't allowed to eat or shit or cry or give birth, nothing goes in, nothing comes out. She takes her clothes off or puts them on, paper doll wardrobe . . . her face twists into poses of exaltation and total abandonment, that is all. She is not bored, she has no other interests. (p. 177)

To the narrator, Anna seems to be an example of the civilized and, therefore, unnatural woman.

Anna's insecurity and emotional weakness are also noticeable in her marriage. She accepts without question that she must follow the rules of the power games David sets up. She is not only a willing player in his games, but when he has affairs, she does the same out of revenge and desperation. By giving in, even reluctantly, to David's demand that she remove her clothes for the film, she invites further abuse.

David

David is the oldest of the group and worries about baldness and putting on weight. A teacher of "Communications" in an adult education program and an ex-radio announcer, he was also once a theology student who sold bibles door-to-door. Like the narrator and Joe, he is an alienated person who never gets close to others. Although he talks a lot, his conversation generally consists of insults, imitations of cartoon characters, and political commentary. He rarely reveals what he really feels. Everything about him seems to be fake. He appears to be a fanatical reactionary, a radical, revolutionary and a nationalist, but in reality he is not.

What at first appears to be charm and humour are later

revealed as vicious weapons used to hurt another person or to establish a position of power. Although he claims to be otherwise, he is more or less an amoral male chauvinist in his dealings with women. He taunts and humiliates Anna and demands that she follow certain rules in their relationship. His lack of feeling for others is seen when he tortures Anna with detailed descriptions of his affairs under the guise of "honesty."

The narrator suspects that, like herself, David cannot love anyone, that "there is something essential missing in us." Beyond his lack of feeling in dealing with others, David, like Anna, is also revealed as a shallow imitation of a human being:

> He was an imposter, a pastiche, layers of political handbills, pages from magazines, *affiches*, verbs and nouns glued on to him and shredding away, the original surface littered with fragments and tatters. In a black suit knocking on doors, young once, even that had been a costume, a uniform; now his hair was falling off and he didn't know what language to use, he'd forgotten his own, he had to copy. Second-hand American was spreading over him in patches, like mange or lichen. He was infested, garbled, and I couldn't help him: it would take such time to heal, unearth him, scrape him down to where he was true. (p. 162-163)

Setting

The setting of *Surfacing* is more than physical background. It helps highlight several of the ideas Atwood has set out to explore. The idea of dualism, two different things opposing one another, occurs throughout the novel, most noticeably in the apparent separation between the narrator's mind and her body or emotions. This pattern of dualism is introduced early in the book in the concepts of city/wilderness, north/south and French/English. As the narrator and her friends set out on their trip, they leave the city and head north. Their destination is a cabin on a secluded island deep in the northern woods. The contrasts between the north and the south and between the city and the wilderness are immediately observable.

The tension between French and English people is also noticeable. The narrator has trouble communicating with people in the French-speaking village and remembers that, even as a child, she felt alienated from them even though she spent so much time there. For her, this area also represents the past, which accounts for her unease as they drive farther away from the city. Her anxiousness is obvious when she refers to the area as "my home ground, foreign territory."

The setting in *Surfacing* is also connected with the journey the characters take. The story opens with an ordinary journey from a southern city to a cabin in the north. This journey, however, also parallels another journey: the trip that the narrator takes into her past and herself. Both journeys are confusing and fearful. As the narrator gets closer to the cabin, she has to stop and ask directions because roads and landmarks have changed. These changes upset her a great deal. The closer she gets to the cabin, the more difficult the journey is and the more upset she becomes. The difficult nature of this journey foreshadows the confusing and complex nature of her personal journey into herself and her past. Several aspects of this landscape also reflect the narrator's anxious state of mind. The boat journey follows a maze-like course where it is very easy to become lost and, similarly, the narrator feels lost and helpless, as if she's walking in circles with no clear idea of the direction she should be heading.

Style

Atwood's experience as a poet can be seen in *Surfacing*. She has a tight control over the prose and through it reinforces and highlights changes in the plot and in the characterization of the narrator. The language Atwood uses in this book reveals things about the narrator because she presents it as if it is the narrator's choice of words. The language is cool, impersonal and precise. It effectively conveys the narrator's cool approach to life and her inability to feel.

As the narrator begins her strange, visionary experience near the end of the book, however, the language begins to change. Atwood avoids the witty comments and the complex and confusing threads of memory found in the first part of the book. The style becomes simpler and at one point — in Chapter 24 when the narrator has an intense vision — Atwood no longer uses periods but uses spaces instead to try and communicate what cannot be spoken. The drastic change in the language reflects the changes in the narrator. The language becomes less complicated and more direct, less intellectual and more emotional, just as the narrator does.

Point of View

Surfacing is narrated from the first person point of view, and the way in which Atwood uses this method of narration is important for a number of reasons. Because it is informal and conversational, this technique lets the reader identify with the narrator. It is as if the narrator is talking directly to us, telling us what is happening, as it is happening. It is also traditionally a very conversational method of narration because diaries and autobiographies are narrated in the first person. The way that Atwood controls the tone of this narration, however, cuts down on the closeness that we might otherwise feel with the narrator. The cool distance of the narrator's voice implies that she is a cold person, and it is difficult for the reader to feel close to such a character. It comes as little surprise to us when the narrator discovers that one of the things she must learn to do is get in touch with her emotions.

Because the story is told by one speaker, the events and characters are seen only through her eyes. What we know and what we feel abut the other characters is determined by how the narrator feels and by how she describes them. The reader receives no second opinions on the actions of the other characters in the novel.

The reader must always keep in mind that some narrators are more reliable than others. It is important not to jump to the conclusion that the narrator is always telling the truth. The speaker in *Surfacing* is shown to be a particularly unreliable narrator. The reader discovers as the story proceeds that the narrator lies not only to others but to herself and to the reader as well. Many of the memories in the first half of the book are not fact but fantasy.

In addition to the actual lies, such as her marriage and the birth of her child, the narrator also reveals a bias that tends to distort reality. Before the reader is made aware of the central lies that the narrator has told about her life, the narrator's confrontation with the "American" fishermen indicates that she distorts things to suit herself. When the fishermen turn out to be Canadians from Sarnia, the narrator doesn't question her judgment but gets angry at them for "disguising" themselves.

Plot

The plot of *Surfacing* follows that of the mystery novel very closely. The mystery novel is one in which mystery or terror plays a major role. Atwood has used elements of the gothic novel — a type of mystery novel — in *Lady Oracle.* In *Surfacing*, she uses the plot of the detective story, widely popularized by novelists such as Agatha Christie in England and Dashiell Hammett in the United States.

In the mystery or detective story there are four important features, and *Surfacing* has each of them. First, there is a disruption of the established order of things. This disruption is a crime, usually a murder, occurring in either the past — before the book begins — or at the beginning of the book. Secondly, the action of the novel is dominated by attempts to reconstruct the events leading up to the present disordered state of things, thereby explaining them. Thirdly, the author generally hides these earlier events, usually by giving only hints or fragments, thereby delaying the reader's ability to recognize the explanation as a whole. Finally, the conclusion of the detective novel is not concerned with the punishment of the guilty person but with the resolution that comes when the events leading to the crime are suddenly seen as complete and whole.

The disappearance of the narrator's father, which occurs before the book begins, and her search for clues as to what has happened to him easily fill the first two requirements. The misleading clues and different explanations for his disappearance that keep emerging and the sudden resolution that comes with the discovery of his body also follow the pattern of the detective novel closely and satisfy the last two requirements.

In following this pattern, Atwood tells a story that is suspenseful and holds the reader's interest. She adds a new twist, however, with the development of two lines of mystery and suspense. The narrator acts like a detective and investigates the truth about and the reasons for the disappearance of her father, which has created a personal crisis for her. She never discovers the total truth about his death; she can only assume that he drowned while photographing Indian rock paintings. Instead, she discovers that such a search can be fearful and confusing.

As she seeks clues that will explain his disappearance, she

unravels the secret of his research. After diving into unknown waters by herself, a dangerous thing to do, she solves two mysteries: the truth about her father's disappearance and the truth about her baby. The discovery of this hidden truth about the abortion is the moment of insight detective novels are famous for. The reader can finally put together all the clues he has been given and can now distinguish between the true and the false explanations that the narrator has provided.

Surfacing is also a detective novel that reveals the limits of such detection and warns that the complete and rational explanations usually found in detective novels are not always found in real life. The narrator dislikes the detective novels that Anna is reading because they create the illusion that with death there is always a logical motive. She comes to realize the dangers of relying too much on rational explanations. She also discovers that life is not so precisely ordered and that guilt and responsibility are often difficult to determine. Once she feels less burdened by the need to discover absolute answers, she becomes less of a dualist. She realizes that life is not black and white; there is not necessarily "a good kind and a bad kind of everything."

Structure

Surfacing follows a simple structural outline. The story unfolds over several days, and we follow the action from morning until night, day after day. The novel is divided into three parts:

Part One:	Chapters 1 to 8
Part Two:	Chapters 9 to 19
Part Three:	Chapters 20 to 27

Dramatically, *Surfacing* is well-balanced in its three part division. The traditional dramatic structure consists of rising action, climax and falling action. Part One introduces the characters and the physical background, and sets in motion the groundwork for the action of the novel. The problem of the disappearance of the narrator's father results in rising action as the narrator searches for clues. Her decision that her father is insane and watching them from the bushes coincides with the group's decision to stay and the section ends on a note of suspense.

Part Two continues to develop the rising action as the search goes on and the narrator discovers that her father was not crazy but was researching rock paintings. The climax and turning point of the book is in Chapter 17 when the narrator discovers the shocking truth about herself and her father's disappearance. Part Three looks at the effects of the climax on the narrator. The action begins to wind down, and Joe's final appearance implies a vague but possible resolution to the dramatic conflict developed in the book.

In addition to being dramatically effective, the three-part structure of *Surfacing* provides a well-balanced framework for the experiences of the narrator. In the first part, the narrator is obsessed by the "sin" she once committed: her abortion. She rejects this sin by constructing a network of deception and lies. It is in this section that she tells the reader of her marriage and divorce and, most importantly, of the existence of her child. It is also in this section that the narrator helps kill living things when she takes Joe and David fishing. Significantly, Part One ends with the narrator on the dock where she pushes herself into the lake. This action signals that a change is going to take place and foreshadows the climatic dive occurring in the next part.

In Part Two, the narrator and her friends discover the dead heron, and she begins to realize that like the Americans who killed the heron, she is also killing things when she goes fishing. This realization upsets her, and she begins to avoid killing anything. With her dive into the water in Chapter 17, the section takes a dramatic turn from the first part. In Part One, she rejected her "sin," now she is forced to acknowledge it. Faced with a vision of her baby, she now sees that she is a killer, too. She must accept that she is not innocent. This section ends with the discovery of her father's body by the Americans, and her refusal to believe it is his. Her final statement, "nothing has died, everything is alive, everything is waiting to become alive," foreshadows both her own rebirth and her pregnancy, which occur in the next part.

Finally, in Part Three, we have other dramatic reversals of situations occurring in the two previous sections, especially Part One. The narrator has gone from rejecting her "sin" to acknowledging it, and now she tries to pay for her "sin" by conceiving a child with Joe. When she is certain she is pregnant, she senses that her lost child is surfacing within her, forgiving her. Her father's gift of sight has occurred in Part Two. The conception of a child is the gift of her mother: how to act. Whereas the narrator had travelled north into the wilderness with great reluctance and fear in Part One, she immerses herself totally with nature in Part Three. Functioning in a mechanical, unfeeling way in Part One, she emerges at the end of Part Three as a total human being, complete with feelings.

Atwood's use of tense in *Surfacing* also complements the three-part structure. The first part is narrated in the present tense. The narrator is telling us what is happening as it is happening. However, the use of the present tense also implies a separation between present and past events, and it helps to reinforce the idea of the narrator as a character who is cut off from her past.

When Atwood switches to the past tense in Part Two, it signals a change in the narrator's perspective. The narrator is re-entering her past, recalling more and more events that happened to her as a child. It is in this section that she examines evidence of her childhood: scrapbooks and photo albums. It is also in this section that she discovers the most important piece of evidence linking to her past: a vision of her child.

With the return to the present tense in Part Three, Atwood signals the return of the narrator to the present. After examining and exploring the past and after having a sense of timelessness while she was experiencing visions, the narrator re-enters the present. She is now able to live in the present because she has gotten in touch with her past. It is no longer isolated from her but a part of her everyday experiences.

Themes

The Quest

There are several themes in *Surfacing*, but two of the most central are the narrator's search for herself or her true identity, and her search for some means of becoming closer to other people. These searches are patterned after the ancient heroic quest, which Joseph Campbell, author of *Hero with a Thousand Faces*, describes as "a separation from the world, a penetration to some source of power, and a life-enhancing return." [1]

In the ancient tales of quests, the hero would make a difficult journey into some dark and unknown region where he would go through many rituals and tests of his strength. In this dark region where unknown forces live, he would gain some special knowledge or experience some form of revelation. When he then returns to the conscious world, he loses the superhuman powers he had attained while on his quest but keeps some parts of the insight he has gained. The most famous examples of this pattern were tales that were told of the quest for the Holy Grail.

The first search, the search for self, is a psychological quest. The narrator's attempt to lessen the alienation between herself and others is a social quest.

The Psychological Quest

In *Surfacing*, Atwood is writing about a search for unity and wholeness in a "divided" person. The first sentence in the book alerts the reader that the work concerns a journey and a search: "I can't believe I'm on this road again." The narrator's division is two-fold. She experiences a division between her mind and her body — or reason and emotion — and between the present and the past. In her search, she concentrates on both these problems, and the resolution she seeks is a sense of wholeness.

Many images of fragmentation and division are found in the book. One important image, describing her sense of inner division, occurs at the beginning of Part Two as she begins to recognize her problem and her need to solve it:

> The trouble is all in the knob at the top of our bodies. I'm not against the body or the head either; only the neck, which creates the illusion that they are separate.

> The language is wrong, it shouldn't have different words for them. If the head extended directly onto the shoulders like a worm's or a frog's without that constriction, that lie, they wouldn't be able to look down at their bodies and move them around as if they were robots or puppets; they would have to realize that if the head is detached from the body both of them will die. (p. 81)

Later, she looks through her mother's photo album to try and discover when this separation took place, but it offers no clues. She realizes she is unable to feel anything and is afraid for her own survival. She is now trying to solve the mystery of her own "death" because "there was the fear that I wasn't alive."

Evidence of her lack of emotion is found in the earlier parts of the book. Immediately following her dive into the water in Chapter 17, however, the narrator's quest moves to another stage. She has looked for clues regarding her division of self and has experienced her first revelation. Significantly, that revelation — the vision of a fetus — is described as a "grail." She senses that "feeling was beginning to seep back into me," and she recognizes that she wanted to be whole again.

The narrator's search has begun to follow the pattern of the quest more closely. She feels she has "power," which helps her recognize things and people for what they are. With the presence of her parents acting as her guides, she now begins the rituals and tests of strength that will allow her to experience more revelations and become a totally unified human being.

The first ritual she undertakes is to have a child. In the days that follow, she becomes conscious of the child within her, and the separation between her mind and her body begins to lessen. One of the most intense rituals she undergoes is the purgation by fire of everything in the cabin that can be burned. This is followed by her going into the water and her removal of her clothes. She senses that these are the tests she must go through in order to experience more revelations.

The vision of her mother is the first revelation after her "sacrifices," and the vision of her father is the second. After these visions, she sees her life more clearly and begins to return to the normal world. She realizes that she loves and trusts Joe and even though things won't be easy, she sees a future for them. She has returned from her quest as a unified human being with reason and emotion working within her.

In searching for her divided self, the narrator must discover and integrate not only her emotional self but her past as well. She must recover some sense of her past if she is to become psychologically whole, since it is largely through looking at our past that we discover who we are.

By returning to the cabin where she spent much of her childhood, she makes her first step towards the discovery of her past. Her memories, childhood scrapbooks and photographs provide some clues. The false history she has created around her "husband" and her child, however, stands in the way of her coming to terms with her past. It is not until after her dive into the lake that she finally accepts the truth about her past. After her dive, she begins to see her past without the distortions and deceptions she had created around it.

Now that the narrator has accepted her past and has integrated a truthful version of it within herself, she understands herself better. There is no longer any need to remain in the cabin — in the past — and she begins planning for her return to the city.

The Social Quest

Although *Surfacing* concentrates upon the experiences of one person, one of the central issues of the book is the relationships between people. The narrator and her friends are alienated people, unable to communicate successfully between themselves. They live isolated and withdrawn lives. In examining the problems of alienation and communication and the narrator's attempts to overcome these problems, *Surfacing* relates a social quest.

By regarding the novel as a psychological quest, it became obvious that the narrator is, at the beginning, alienated from herself. However, she is alienated from other people as well — Joe, David and Anna, and her parents. In turn, these people suffer from the same problem.

The alienation of the narrator is shown in a number of ways. She has a variety of disruptions in her personal relationships, which is made worse by communication problems. The barriers that she sets up between herself and others can be seen in the use of pronouns. She remains nameless throughout the book, referring to herself only as "I." She never reveals the names of her father, mother, brother or her "husband," referring to them as "they." Her world is divided between herself and others, "I" and "they."

She and her friends know very little about each other. Even though she considers Anna her best friend, the narrator does not seem to know or understand her. Anna tries to make deeper contact with her, but the narrator avoids any closeness.

The narrator is also alienated from her family. She is out of touch with her brother and had stopped visiting her family several years ago. Aside from her lack of communication with them, the narrator's parents are presented as being very withdrawn and alienated people. The narrator recalls her mother taking long walks alone and her closest relationship was with the bluejays that lived near the cabin. Her father was, in many ways, anti-social. He withdrew from society, and his family lived for half the year in different cities and the other half on a remote island. Cut off from people for such long periods of time, it does not seem surprising that the narrator's family all had difficulty in making contact with others.

Like the narrator's mother, Joe is another alienated person who prefers silence to speech. He and the narrator rarely talk, and she is never sure what he is thinking or feeling. Their relationship also suffers from her almost total lack of commitment. When Joe breaks his usual silence and proposes, she becomes suspicious. His former silence had allowed her to avoid any kind of commitment between them because it made no demands upon her.

She becomes more and more withdrawn from her friends and grows suspicious of language and the way it can distort. Finally, she chooses physical isolation — a voluntary seclusion from society and gets rid of anything human about herself, becoming more and more like an animal.

She moves to a non-verbal level and explores other means of communication. She feels "the names of things fading but their forms and uses remaining," and English words begin to sound "imported, foreign."

With the end of her visionary experience, she realizes that she is no longer an animal and has become human again. Since human beings are social by nature, she realizes that she must rejoin society. With the return to society is also the return to language since it is needed for communication and the development of relationships between people. She recognizes that her relationship with Joe will be difficult, but they can no longer lock themselves inside their silences.

1. Joseph Campbell, *Hero With A Thousand Faces*. (New York: Meridian, 1949) p. 143.

Social Commentary

Surfacing is a very political book — not surprising since Margaret Atwood is one of the most outspoken novelists in Canada. Although a strong nationalist herself, Atwood spends much of her time in the book making fun of ineffective and misguided nationalism. Through the character of David, she attacks those so-called nationalists who simply spout political slogans and sayings that mean nothing. David's political activity is limited to repeating phrases like "rotten capitalist bastards." When he describes his theory of the approaching war between the Canadian nationalist guerrilla movement and the "Yanks," the narrator realizes that the guerrillas would never even make it through a winter. Because of their lack of knowledge and experience of the countryside, they would die of starvation and exposure.

In her critical study of Canadian literature, *Survival*, Atwood states that people often seek out the victim role as a way of escaping responsibility. The narrator, for instance, avoids moral responsibility for the death of her child by presenting herself as the victim of a failed marriage. In nationalistic terms, people like David, and the narrator as well, may easily avoid responsibility for their country's destruction of its natural resources by seeing Canada as a victim of the United States. It never seems to be Canadians who are over-hunting or over-fishing, or otherwise destroying the balance of nature in *Surfacing*, only the "Americans." The narrator comes to see that this is not so. The "Americans" who killed the heron turn out to be Canadians, and it is Canadians who want to flood the lake and destroy many of the trees surrounding it. The narrator must accept that she and her country are just as responsible for the destruction of the environment as the Americans are.

Finally, Atwood also becomes a social critic in her use of anti-Americanism in *Surfacing*. When the narrator discovers that the men responsible for the senseless killing of the heron are Canadians, she says that "it doesn't matter what country they're from, they're still Americans." American comes to mean not just someone from the United States. The narrator re-defines the word as meaning 20th century, technological, modern man. American comes to represent anyone who is alienated from nature, and when she senses that her friends are becoming like robots, she begins to feel that they are becoming "Americans." As far as she is concerned, "if you look like them and talk like them and think like them then you are them." To be an American is to kill for sport or destroy without any understanding or guilt about what you have destroyed. To be an American is to be unable to understand that we must treat the universe with care because nature is sacred. The anti-Americanism in *Surfacing* is not directed against the United States but against those people who are destroying the planet.

Symbolism and Imagery

A symbol is something that is itself and yet stands for something else. A common example of this would be a flag, which is a piece of cloth that also stands for a nation. As it applies to criticism, symbol refers to a word or phrase that combines a literal quality with an abstract or suggestive aspect. In this sense, the word "cross" has a literal quality in that it means two pieces of wood joined together. It also has an abstract quality in that it has a meaning beyond itself: the cross suggests the suffering of Christ and suffering or sacrifice in general. Symbols may be conventional, such as the cross or the white dove — which symbolizes peace — gaining their meaning from references in history, religion or folklore. Symbols may also be private, developed within a book. The most obvious example of this in *Surfacing* would be the symbol of the fish.

In criticism, it is important to know the difference between symbols and imagery. Imagery consists of images, metaphors and similes. Imagery refers to a concrete object and functions to describe that object. A symbol does the same thing except that it goes beyond describing the object by making it suggest a meaning beyond itself.

Symbolism

The symbols in *Surfacing* work to support the themes. Of the four main symbols, two are conventional, drawing their power from traditional associations, and two are private, drawing their power from the importance they gain as the novel proceeds. All four symbols are part of the story on a literal level, while working very strongly on a symbolic level.

While images of separation and dualism are common in *Surfacing*, one symbol comes to represent the idea of unity or wholeness: the fish. Fish appear frequently in *Surfacing*. The narrator and her friends go fishing several times and they meet up with other fishermen. One of the Indian paintings the narrator refers to is that of a figure resembling a fish. For the narrator, the fish begins to symbolize wholeness, the unity between mind and body that she is seeking. Fish, like frogs, snakes or worms, have heads that extend directly into the shoulders, thereby making it more difficult to see their heads and their bodies as separate. The narrator begins to dislike killing of fish because they represent for her the goal of unity: "neckless headbody, the fish is whole."

The heron is both a conventional and private symbol in *Surfacing*. Significantly, the narrator herself notes the first symbolic role that herons play in the novel: "once people believed the flight of the birds was an [omen]." Just as folklore indicates that birds may be omens — signs of what is about to occur — so the herons in *Surfacing* take on this predictive role. The narrator sees herons flying overhead on two occasions before her traumatic dive into the water.

When the narrator discovers the mutilated body of a heron, the importance of herons as omens grows. In addition, the heron begins to symbolize suffering. She later remembers the living and the dead heron: "unsacred cross, the shape of the heron flying above us the first evening we fished, a bluegrey cross, and the other heron or was it the same one, hanging wrecked from the tree." The first heron predicted the death of the second and the second heron comes to symbolize suffering as the narrator makes repeated allusions to Christ on the cross. The second heron also comes to symbolize man's senseless exploitation of nature since it is neither a source of food nor a dangerous creature. Significantly, the heron, like the Golden Phoenix, is also a traditional symbol of regeneration and rebirth and thus points to both the narrator's suffering and her eventual rebirth.

Two aspects of the natural world, water and air, work together to provide powerful symbols. They support and highlight the narrator's psychological quest into herself. The symbols of water and air draw upon their traditional associations: air is associated with consciousness or reason and water is associated with the unconscious or feeling.

The narrator is suffering from a psychological block between these two areas. She has repressed or denied the abortion she has had, and psychologists say that repressed material moves from the conscious part of the mind into the unconscious. When the narrator first dives into the water at the end of Part One, she says that "finally being in the air is more painful than being in the water and I bend and push myself reluctantly into the lake." Even though her descent into her unconscious and its hidden material is painful and dangerous, it is also necessary. Significantly, the narrator reinforces the symbolic implications of water and air by frequently referring to waking up or coming out from under the influence of anesthesia as "surfacing."

When she dives into the lake in Chapter 17, she sees the body of her father. However, this body appears to her as the body of the child she aborted, the memory of which she has repressed. Thus, on a symbolic level, she leaves the conscious world for the unconscious world and encounters there the memories and fears that have been hidden from consciousness. When she returns to the air, surfacing, she returns to the conscious world. It is after this return from the unconscious that the narrator's psychological problems start to heal, and she begins to feel emotions again. *Surfacing* is a book about both diving and surfacing — entering the unconscious and returning to consciousness — and these two symbols highlight the two aspects of this central concern.

Imagery

Surfacing has a large network of images that gain greater importance as the story proceeds. Unlike most of the symbols in the book, these images are not taken from history, religion or folklore but take their meaning from the narrator's personal associations with them. The imagery of *Surfacing* helps develop characterization, direct the plot and reinforces the main ideas and themes.

The images, similes and metaphors that the narrator chooses to describe other people reveal a great deal about the character of both the narrator and of others. Joe, for instance, is constantly compared to animals. David, on the other hand, is becoming bald and seems to chatter non-stop. David and Anna are described by the narrator as being like robots or machines. Such passages go beyond being simple description. They reveal as much about the narrator as the person she is describing because she is saying how these people are perceived by her. David and Anna are, of course, not robots, but they seem to be from the narrator's perspective. In addition, almost all of the imagery describing the characters can be divided into two groups: the natural and the unnatural or technological. To compare Joe to an animal or her mother to a bird reflects their positive aspects; to compare David and Anna to machines reflects their negative aspects.

Other images that appear throughout the book are connected to plot and theme. Images of fragmentation or dismemberment, such as the narrator's memory of the storekeeper who was missing a hand, recur frequently in *Surfacing*. They reinforce the idea of the narrator's separation of her head from her body, one of the central ideas of the book.

Also present in the novel are images of death and decay. The natural setting includes rotting logs in the water, decomposing leaves in the forest, and the cabin and the surrounding docks, sheds and garden are all in a state of decay. The narrator has memories of both her mother's death and the animals her brother allowed to die after capturing them. These images can be linked to the rediscovery of her child's "death" and her discovery of her father's death. They also highlight the emotional "death" that has taken place within the narrator.

Finally, images of imprisonment are also found in *Surfacing*. Again, one of the narrator's strongest memories of her brother is of his trapping frogs and crayfish and putting them in bottles and cans. Later, she discovers while looking through her mother's photo album that pictures can freeze people, and she feels herself as a child "shut behind the paper." David and Joe's film also imprisons people:

> The film coils onto the sand under the water, weighted down by its containers; the invisible captured images are swimming away into the lake like tadpoles, Joe and David beside their defeated log, axemen, arms folded, Anna with no clothes on jumping off the end of the dock, finger up, hundreds of tiny naked Annas no longer bottled and shelved. (p. 178)

The narrator also feels that the mirror traps her and thinks of "Anna's soul closed in the gold compact." All of these images can be linked to the problem of the narrator's imprisoned self. She has shut away her feelings and her past and must learn to release both. She also must learn how to release herself from the imprisonment of her guilt over her abortion.

In addition, the images of mirrors and cameras reinforce

the idea of the stealing of identity or, as the narrator puts it, of the soul. Anna's identity or soul is locked in the gold compact because she cannot express herself for fear that David will reject her. The desire to capture images with a camera proved fatal for the narrator's father since he seemed to have died while trying to photograph Indian rock paintings. His body is not discovered for some time because it is weighted down by the camera around his neck.

Selected Criticisms

The title of Atwood's novel, *Surfacing*, suggests its theme: a swimmer surfaces so that air, not water, will fill her lungs. Surfacing, then, is a metaphor for rebirth, awakening, return. But one cannot come up without first diving down; and most of the novel is concerned with downward movement. An unnamed woman, the narrator and central character, dives into human history, into her personal past, and into her own psyche. From concealed depths of the self, from a level of feeling beyond the reach of words or reasons — from a place the world calls madness — the woman emerges into the world with a new vision of herself and of her powers as a human being.

Joan Larkin, "Soul Survivor," *Ms.*

You could call it an adventure thriller set in the wilds of northern Quebec. You could call it a detective story centering on the search for the main character's missing father. You could call it a psychological novel, a study of madness both individual and social. You could call it a religious novel which examines the origin and nature of the human lust to kill and destroy. You could call it any of these and I wouldn't quarrel. But you'd better call it a novel to be reckoned with, a step in the direction of that mythic creature, the Great Canadian Novel.

Patricia Morley, "Multiple Surfaces," *Urchin*

I've read *Surfacing* a couple of times now, and I'm still convinced that it's one of the best novels we've ever had; that, despite its few flaws, and it does have a few, it says so much about our condition now, in such a trenchant and truly memorable manner, and does it all in a narrative of such power, that we can only give thanks that we're so lucky as to have Margaret Atwood around to write books like this for us. Aside from anything else, *Surfacing* is a superb literary experience, a truly exciting story, one you'll have trouble putting down until you're finished.

Douglas Barbour, *Book Reviews*

For me the novel is a social vehicle. It reflects society. Serious writers these days don't write uplifting books because what they see around them is not uplifting. It would be hypocritical to say the world is inspirational. It's not. These days the world is a pretty dismal place. You can blank that out. You can destroy your Amnesty International newsletter without reading it. But that doesn't make that stuff go away. The less you pay attention to it, the more it's going to be there for somebody else.

Margaret Atwood in *For Openers: Conversations With 24 Canadian Writers*, by Alan Twigg

I think ever since we all left the Roman Catholic Church we've defined ourselves as innocent in one way or another. But what I'm really into in [*Surfacing*] is the . . . great Canadian victim complex. If you define yourself as innocent then nothing is ever your fault — it is always somebody else doing it to you, and until you stop defining yourself as a victim that will always be true. It will always be somebody else's fault, and you will always be the object of that rather than somebody who has any choice or takes responsibility for their life. And that is not only the Canadian stance towards the world, but the usual female one. Look at what a mess I am and it's all their fault. And Canadians do that too. Look at poor innocent us, we are morally better than they. We do not burn people in Vietnam, and those bastards are coming in and taking our country. Well the real truth of the matter is that Canadians are selling it.

Margaret Atwood in *Eleven Canadian Novelists*, by Graeme Gibson

If the only two kinds of people are killers and victims, then although it may be morally preferable to be a victim, it is obviously preferable from the point of view of survival to be a killer. However either alternative seems pretty hopeless; you know, you can define yourself as an innocent and get killed, or you can define yourself as a killer and kill others. I think there has to be a third thing again; the ideal would be somebody who would neither be a killer nor a victim, who could achieve some kind of harmony with the world, which is a productive or creative harmony, rather than a destructive relationship towards the world.

Margaret Atwood in *Eleven Canadian Novelists*, by Graeme Gibson

The unnamed narrator in Atwood's novel struggles to resolve problems of self through a quest for meaningful identity. If she can discover who she is, she can perhaps cope with what she has become. The violence that has been worked upon her personality, a good deal of it sexual and of her own doing in response to the society around her, may be absolved through recognition of her place in the larger scheme of things. The keys to such knowledge prove elusive, however, being in the possession of her dead mother and father and the primeval and prenatal past of the species. She must first cross over the boundaries of what is regarded as normal experience into intensified perceptual and conceptual consciousness, called madness by some and, by others, visionary insight. Ultimately she returns to conditional sanity. There is nowhere else to go.

John Moss, *Sex and Violence in the Canadian Novel: The Ancestral Present*

The themes are many, and the nature of reality is one of the most interesting. Some of the themes concern our most burning contemporary issues — the role of women, the facts of urban life, and most of all, the wounding and perhaps killing of our only home, Earth. Margaret Atwood is one of the very few novelists writing today who can deal with these issues without ever writing propaganda. Perhaps she has been able to do this partly because she has interwoven all these themes with the theme which is central to our mythology, our religion, our history and (whether we know it or not) our hearts — humankind's quest for the archetypal parents, for our gods, for our own meanings in the face of our knowledge of the inevitability of death.

Margaret Laurence, *Quarry.* 22, No. 2 (Spring 1973)

Surfacing is no novel of escape, but a parable to demonstrate not only the necessity of making some kind of choice, but the even greater importance of facing the truth, first and foremost. This is a powerful novel that absorbs the reader far beyond the last printed page.

Isobel McKenna, *The Town & Country,* Dec. 13, 1972

The need not to be a victim, the need to start over despite the probability of failure, the need for human interaction and, underneath it all, the need to grow. These things that need to be said are said in [*Surfacing* in] a way that makes you remember.

Reg Smith, *The Gauntlet*, Dec. 6, 1972

Suggested Study Topics

1. *Surfacing* describes a woman's search for identity. In what way can this search be regarded as parallel to Canada's attempt to discover its national identity?

2. Choose two characters and describe how images of nature and images of technology are used to portray their personalities.

3. How do tense changes relate to the development of plot in *Surfacing*?

4. Discuss the differences between the narrator's mother and father. What do they come to represent to the narrator during her visionary experiences?

5. Atwood is concerned with social issues. Discuss her treatment in *Surfacing* of nationalism and ecology.

6. Examine the problems the reader encounters with Atwood's use of the first person narrator.

7. Discuss Atwood's portrayal of the relationships between men and women.

8. What does the narrator learn about the problems language poses as a means of communication? How does she resolve these problems?

Bibliography

Anderson, Paula. "Some Thoughts about Margaret Atwood." *White Pelican* 4, No. 1 (Winter 1974).

Ayre, John. "Margaret Atwood and the End of Colonialism." *Saturday Night* (September 1972).

Bastian, D.G. "Life Since Atwood." *Vic Report* 10, No. 1 (Fall 1981).

Bjerring, Nancy E. "The Problem of Language in Margaret Atwood's *Surfacing*." *Queen's Quarterly* 3, No. 1 (Winter 1976).

Brown, Russell M. "Atwood's Sacred Wells." *Essays on Canadian Writing* No. 17 (Spring 1980).

Campbell, Joseph. *Hero With A Thousand Faces.* New York: Meridian, 1949.

Christ, Carol. "Refusing to be Victim: Margaret Atwood." *Diving Deep and Surfacing* Boston: Beacon Press, 1980.

Clery, Val. "A Plea for Victims." *Books in Canada* 1, No. 12 (Nov/Dec. 1972).

Conlon, Patrick. "Margaret Atwood: Beneath the Surface." *Toronto Life* (Feb. 1975).

Craig, James. "In Spite of all That." *Vancouver Sun* (Nov. 9, 1972).

Davey, Frank. *From There to Here: A Guide to English-Canadian Literature Since 1960.* Erin: Press Porcepic, 1974.

______. "Atwood Walking Backwards." *Open Letter* No. 5.

Dobbs, Kildare. "Canadian's Second Novel Even Better Than Her First." *Toronto Star* (Sept. 12, 1972).

Eliade, Mircea. *The Sacred and the Profane: The Nature of Religion.* New York: Harcourt, Brace and World, 1957.

Freedman, Adele. "Happy Heroine and 'Freak' of Canadian Literature." *Toronto Globe and Mail.* (Oct. 25, 1980).

French, William. "Resurfacing." *Toronto Globe and Mail.*

Fulford, Robert. "Do Canadians Fear Excellence?" *Saturday Night* (May 1980)

Gabori, Susan. "Beginnings." *Today Magazine* (March 29, 1980).

Galt, George. "*Surfacing* and the Critics." *Canadian Forum* 54, No. 640-641 (May/June 1974).

Gibson, Graeme. *Eleven Canadian Novelists.* Toronto: House of Anansi Press, 1973.

Gibson, M.E. "Interview with Margaret Atwood." *Chicago Review* 27, No. 4 (Spring 1976).
Hammond, Karla. "An Interview with Margaret Atwood." *The American Poetry Review* 8, No. 5 (Sept. 1979).
Harcourt, Joan. "Atwood Country." *Queen's Quarterly* 80 No. 2 (Summer 1973).
Harrison, James. "The 20,000,000 Solitudes of *Surfacing*." *Dalhousie Review* 1, No. 1 (Spring 1979).
Klinck, Carl, ed. *Literary History of Canada*. Toronto: University of Toronto Press, 1977.
Laurence, Margaret. [book review of *Surfacing*] *Quarry* 22, No. 2 (Spring 1973).
Lyons, Boonie. "Neither Victim Nor Executioners in Margaret Atwood's *Surfacing*." *World Literature Written in English* 17, No. 1 (April 1978).
MacGregor, Roy. "Atwood's World." *Maclean's* (Oct. 1979).
McLay, Catherine. "The Divided Self: Theme and Pattern in *Surfacing*." *The Canadian Novel Here and Now*. John Moss, ed. Toronto: NC Press, 1976.
Mandel, Eli. *Another Time*. Erin: Press Porcepic, 1971.
Mansbridge, Francis. "Search for Self in the Novels of Margaret Atwood." *Journal of Canadian Fiction* No. 22 (1978).
Miner, Valerie. "The Many Facets of Margaret Atwood." *Chatelaine* (June 1975).
Morris, Ken. "Survival in the Writing of Margaret Atwood." *Cross Country* No. 1 (Winter 1975).
Moss, John. *Sex and Violence in the Canadian Novel: The Ancestral Present*. Toronto: McClelland & Stewart, 1977.
Northey, Margot. *The Haunted Wilderness: The Gothic and Grotesque in Canadian Fiction*. Toronto: University of Toronto Press, 1976.
Oates, Joyce Carol. "A Conversation with Margaret Atwood," *Ontario Review* No. 9 (Fall/Winter 1978-1979).
Rogers, Linda. "Margaret the Magician." *Canadian Literature* No. 60 (Spring 1974).
Rosenberg, Jerome. "Woman as Everyman in Atwood's *Surfacing*." *Studies in Canadian Literature* 3, No. 1 (Winter 1978).
Ross, Catherine. "Nancy Drew as Shaman." *Canadian Literature* No. 84 (Spring 1980).

Schaeffer, Susan. "It is Time That Separates Us: Margaret Atwood's *Surfacing*." *Centennial Review* 18, No. 4 (Fall 1974).

Slinger, Helen. "Interview with Margaret Atwood." *Maclean's* 89, No. 15 (Sept. 6, 1976).

Stanley, Don. "She Discovers Better Gods." *Vancouver Sun* (Nov. 9, 1972).

Tesher, Ellie. "Atwood Surfaces." *Toronto Star* (May 19, 1978).

Toye, William, ed. *Supplement to the Oxford Guide to Canadian History and Literature*. Toronto: Oxford University Press, 1973.

Twigg, Alan. *For Openers: Conversations with 24 Canadian Writers*. Toronto: Harbour Publishing, 1981.

van Varseveld, Gail. "Talking with Atwood." *Room of One's Own* 1, No. 2 (Summer 1975).

White, Kayce. "What She Does is Write." *Vancouver Sun* (March 29, 1975).

Woodcock, George. "Surfacing to Survive." *Ariel* 4, No. 3 (July 1973).

NOTES

NOTES

NOTES

NOTES

NOTES

NOTES

NOTES

NOTES

NOTES

NOTES